# The World
# Is Full
# of It

BOOKS BY

# Isadore Barmash

**NONFICTION**

*The World Is Full of It*

*Welcome to Our Conglomerate
—You're Fired!*

*The Self-Made Man*

**FICTION**

*Net Net*

**ANTHOLOGY**

*Great Business Disasters*

# Isadore Barmash

HOW WE ARE OVERSOLD,
OVERINFLUENCED,
AND OVERWHELMED BY
THE COMMUNICATIONS
MANIPULATORS.

# The World Is Full of It

DELACORTE PRESS
NEW YORK

Designed by Joel Schick

Manufactured in the United States of America

First printing

LIBRARY OF CONGRESS CATALOGING IN PUBLICATION DATA

Barmash, Isadore.
    The world is full of it.
    1. Mass media—Social aspects—United States.
2. United states—Social conditions—1960–
3. Advertising—United States. I. Title.
HN90.M3B37      659.2      73–13632

ISBN: 0-440-09726-6

TO MY FATHER

**Samuel Barmash**

IN FOND MEMORY

# Table

# of

# Contents

*The Premise as a Foreword*

# I. The Argument

# II. Foisting the Fantasy as Reality

# III. The Communicators and the Press

# IV. The Manipulated Society

# The World Is Full of It

# The
# Premise as
# a Foreword

IN AMERICA, circa the 1970s, there is much that is observed but not seen; much that is seen but not understood; much that would be understood if it were not confused, diverted and channeled; much that is confused, diverted and channeled perhaps as much by the recipient's own will as by the manipulator. Could it be that our eyes, ears and comprehension are veiled by our own internal preconditioning and then played to by commercial and power-driven subterfuges? Instead of enjoying truth, are we living out an hourly and daily fantasy, responding to the wrong things for the wrong reasons because of wrong stimuli? If not, then how

© xiii

many of us in an age of instant electronic and computerized communications really knows what is going on all around us?

That, in all audacity, is what this book is about. The premise will be examined, pushed and harassed from both its pro and con aspects by the presentation of a variety of viewpoints gathered in eighteen months of interviews. The goal will be to stimulate the reader's awareness and to provide some measure of defense. Why? So that he will not allow his own subconscious desires, psychic, emotional and economic needs to be used against him by the communications and value manipulators as much in the future as they have been in the present and past.

ISADORE BARMASH

# I.

## The
## Argument

# 1.

## Deception
## and
## Delusion

### A VAST PLOY

ON ANY DAY, the weather; the circumstances and the mood notwithstanding, the barrage on our credibility is constant, pervasive and relentless.

A politician speaks to us in unctuous, confident tones of patriotism tinged with warning. But the fingers of fear flicker at us behind the smiling voice.

An advertiser bombards us with sales pitches that hint at our needs but sell sex, glamour, materialism. At the core of his spiel is hypocrisy, the lies submerged under the whipped cream of sensualness.

From the Mai Lai massacre to the Watergate scandals to the Equity Funding Insurance fraud, from the illegal campaign contributions involving both political parties to the latest West Point cheating incidents to the most recent bribe and kickback disclosures in more and more cities, the integrity of our institutions seems to be crumbling. Are they unable to enjoy prosperity, peace and power without corrupting themselves?

Children grow quickly from infancy to puberty before the television set. One tiny, growing hand turns the dial, the other alternates spasmodically at the vitamin bottle and at a pile of rainbow-colored amphetamines. TV is the new cradle. The hand that rocked it is at Jack LaLanne's.

The proselytizers of the world grab at our vitals. One frightens with the forecasts of doom, another lifts our hopes with the promise of paradise here and now, a third makes it plain that a trusting voice is a trusting heart, a fourth . . .

The communications practitioners—that whole professional bunch of advertising men, public-relations men, sales promoters and just plain paid hustlers—further the process of sell, oversell and victimize by delusion and try to sustain the process endlessly. They *know* us, they convince their clients, they *know* what we will do and say. And they usually do because we help them.

The entertainment and culture communicators find us an easy target. Their selling effort is greased by our eager celebrity worship. Streisand, Taylor, Burton, Sinatra, Bernstein, Carson, Dylan can do no wrong, but even when they do, so what? Talent and personality magnified electronically are tantamount to superhuman—even superstar? And so the entertainers, the celebrities, carry their credibility before them like a proud banner. And we smile happily as they unfurl it.

And we, the recipients of all this, we look at one another, swallow our honesty and deny any misgivings, and play a mutual game of deception. Don't expose yourself too much—that is the truism of the time—you just might be impaled on your own confidences, even be violated, killed or, worst of all, ridiculed.

Thus it is in these days of the final third of the twentieth century. Everywhere, we listen, we see, we hear, we agree, we understand. And we listen not at all, see little, hear less, agree because we are afraid not to and do not understand.

Faced by duplicity on all sides, inflicted with both inner and outer doubts, most of us can't and don't really know what is going on in front of our eyes and within hearing range. How can we when we are both the subjects and the sources of a constant barrage of incredibility?

The heads of our institutions, angered and confused, grope vainly at the tendrils of truth. And the effort sometimes is tinged with humor and even farce.

Recently, Paul Rand Dixon, the bluff former chairman and later a member of the Federal Trade Commission, admitted, "I don't understand the difference between being persuaded and being manipulated." And facetiously but candidly, *Advertising Age* told him: "That's easy. Manipulate is what other people do."

After the FTC hearings on deceptive advertising began in 1971, Dan Seymour, president of J. Walter Thompson, Inc., the world's largest advertising agency, called on his fellow admen to prepare ads and commercials that would extol the positive aspects of advertising. Seymour also asked magazine publishers and radio and television stations to carry free messages. "Perhaps it's time we did for ourselves," he declared straight-faced, "what we did for Smokey the Bear."

Dean Acheson, the acerbic late secretary of state, was not feeling particularly charitable when he observed, "On one thing only I feel a measure of assurance—on the rightness of contempt for sanctimonious self-righteousness which joined with a sly worldliness beclouds the dangers and opportunities of our time with an unctuous film."

It was hardly with a sense of forgiveness that a retired police reporter recalled to this writer the strange antics of two New York civil-court judges who relished a reputation for toughness. Before announcing their judgments, they would scan the courtroom to see which media were there. If a *New York Times* reporter were present, they would add two more years to the sentence.

Candor rather than hypocrisy was evident in another situation. After a *Time* magazine communications seminar by its advertising staff for one of its major advertisers and his advertising agency, an executive of the advertiser turned to an agency executive and wanted to know, "Is it my imagination—or was eighty-five percent of that bullshit?" The adman recoiled momentarily, then grinned and replied, "Isn't eighty-five percent of everything bullshit?"

In a cemetery, as some ghoulish pundit put it, there is total communication. In a mental institution, there is total non-communication. But in our live and sane world of the seventies, there is nothing as pure as either. Instead, our society seems increasingly to function in a self-induced and accepted communications behavior consisting consciously and unconsciously of sham, lies, posturing, image-making and a vast ploy of hoodwink.

Everywhere and on all levels—government, business, society, the home, the school, the club, culture and entertainment, and perhaps especially in relations between people—Americans are engaged in a game of delusion. The goal, instinctive and completely self-protective, is to exaggerate and to mask, to define in terms other than the actual ones that which our senses absorb, our brains conceive and our emotions react to.

If the world is truly "full of it . . ." the implied word missing in the phrase is of course obvious. It is almost a euphemism for what has come to replace truth and straightforwardness, traits that seem to have evaporated in the pressure cooker of contemporary society. This is not so much merely by public default as by equal parts of simple malaise, resignation, a childish seeking to raise heroic structures and figures in every walk of life, a naive glorification of the boons of technology and an explosion of the sources of information and opinion, with all their attendant confusion.

Thus, at a time when America is "enjoying" its first trillion-dollar economy, when personal affluence has reached its peak, when education has unfolded to millions formerly deprived of a full measure, when a so-called new era of enlightened culture has opened, when books pour from the presses in an unprecedented flow, when racial strife has calmed or at least reached some more hopeful plateau, when the country's foreign en-

tanglements have settled to a semblance of noninvolve-
ment, when the public welfare in its medical, mental
health and subsistence needs appears to be making its
greatest strides, when the demands of youth, age and
feminism have come more into their own than ever
before, when sober appraisal of the individual's role in
the texture of society would seem not only invited but
necessitated, we have not reacted either humanely or
honestly to one another nor have our institutions responded with sincerity or integrity to new challenges or
the need for candor. Instead, we have become involved
in a nationally pervasive flimflam.

## THE PLAYS OF THE PLOY

In the seventies, the com-
munications hypocrisy was surfacing in many ways,
seemingly everywhere. Some of the media were on top
of it while many were contributing to it. The government, at once both the instigator and the investigator,
was feinting catlike with it, much to the discomfiture of
the communicators. Business was flagrantly practicing
it while protesting the unfair attacks against the practice. The communications pros, feeling themselves on
the griddle, went about their normal business—which
was conducting hypocritical communications and
wearing a dogmatic expression. And the public, confused and beginning to be aroused, was speaking tartly
to Louis Harris, Gallup and the other takers of the general pulse.

Here are a few, authentic examples of the oversell

and the hypocrisy practiced on the public, all in the name of advertising, merchandising and publicity, all forms of communications:

*Sex and Smoke on the S.S. Ellandem.* More awake subway riders in New York were recently confronted by an interesting, if not disturbing advertising placard. Advertising L&M cigarettes, the large display card proclaimed, "Relax. . . . This is the L&M moment." On a cruise ship, cutely named the S.S. *Ellandem,* a young couple in swimming attire sat intimately on the ship's deck, staring meaningfully into each other's eyes. Her right thigh was lifted in a warmly casual way while his torso was turned one-quarter in her direction so that they smiled with desire at each other, flank to flank, poised cigarette to poised cigarette. Underneath, the ad carried the required surgeon general's warning that cigarette smoking is dangerous to one's health. Can sex offset the cancer threat? The advertiser apparently thought so. What the subway riders thought may be something else again.

*Recalls Not from Detroit.* We all know about the recalls of many thousands of automobiles for defects and safety hazards. But did you ever hear about the recall of 3 million cans of Coca-Cola, Sprite and Fanta soft drinks, or the recall of 200,000 soup bowls by Campbell's Soup for exceeding maximum levels for toxic lead and cadmium? Probably not, for these recalls got very little publicity.

*Mouth-to-Mouth Hysteria.* Recently, a customer phoned a New York department store to order a cabinet that had been advertised. After some incessant ringing, a clerk answered, and when the customer told him what she wanted, he said, "Just a minute, please. I'm waiting on another customer." The phone shopper waited and waited, hanging on to the phone. Finally, a voice came on at the store's end, "Hello, hello." The customer said, "Who are you?" The voice said, "I'm a customer. Who are you?" The first customer said, "Why are you talking on the phone?" The second customer replied, "Well, I've been here waiting for a salesclerk. I saw the phone off the hook and I thought that if I picked it up I might get some help." "What's the problem?" asked the first customer. Both customers told each other of their frustrations and commiserated with each other until they broke up in hysterical laughter.

*Star-Chamber Repression.* If the public was troubled in the early seventies by the unauthorized publication of the Vietnam papers on the U.S. involvement in Indochina, the question of the public's right to know soon spread from Washington and New York to the boondocks. A muzzle was being applied in more than one city hall. In many a town and city in the enlightened seventies, legislators, civic officials and others were anxiously withholding unfavorable news from the press and the public. Reporters, particularly, were running up against star-chamber legislative hearings, withheld records, closed meetings of the town council, "executive" sessions and the like. And the entire effort was complicated by an indifferent public which finally acted only when and if some particular group of citizens happened to become involved.

*Make It Seem Like Something.* "You can't quote me, of course," said one of the country's best-known consumer analysts, "because if you do I'll lose at least half of my clients. But I'm afraid there is an enormous flimflam in the broad area of consumer protection. It's become stylish to give in to the need to *seem* to do something for the consumer. Many corporations establish consumer affairs departments which are at best cosmetic and more often are not even that."

*Pulling the Plug on "Plugola."* Stirring a brouhaha that lasted for weeks, the White House in the person of Clay T. Whitehead, director of the White House Office of Telecommunications Policy, told broadcasters that legislation had been drafted that would hold individual television stations accountable, at the risk of losing their licenses, for the content of all network material they broadcast. In an Indianapolis speech in December 1972, he condemned "ideological plugola" in network-news reporting and warned local stations that they would have to bear responsibility for such matter carried over their facilities. The threat launched months of debate that finally trickled away unresolved when newer issues took precedence.

*Child-Beating.* The Federal Trade Commission, aroused by deceptive advertising, held some five weeks of hearings in late 1971 for "informational" purposes. After listening to eighty witnesses, the agency said that it had reassured itself there was a continuing need for regulation of TV advertising. But what really emerged from the millions of words was the tube's impact on children. Concern was expressed over the effect of child-oriented commercials on the eating habits of children. Will kids grow up to be obese, diabetic vitamin-poppers? This fear arose from the fact that sugar-coated cereals, other sweets and candy-coated vitamins are being extensively advertised to the highly impressionable young audience.

*Hollywood Outpost.* Recently, in pursuit of my research, I asked three of New York's most skillful public-relations men to meet with me in a frank discussion. After dwelling on a wide range of specifics and agreeing that (1) the government was conducting its business by public relations because (2) the public seems to demand labels or identifiable symbols, sympathetic or otherwise; they seemed to get a great charge out of pinpointing the models that had emerged in the White House. So Eisenhower was Daddy Warbucks (from the Little Orphan Annie comic strip), Cary Grant was in the White House in the guise of John F. Kennedy, Lyndon Johnson was Hopalong Cassidy, Harry Truman was Wild Bill Hickok and Nixon was—well, Nixon was Nixon, or maybe John Wayne. When I assailed the trio for being indirectly responsible for the PR image making that resulted in such simplistic models, they shrugged. One summed up the group's view: "Whaddaya want? The public demands a hero or a villain. If they've seen too many movies, whose fault is it?"

PR *for* JVL? In 1972 and early 1973, when New York City seemed to be going to hell on a bicycle, the role of Mayor John V. Lindsay appeared to be fluid. After a controversial record as mayor and an unsuccessful try in the 1972 presidential primary, Lindsay had not quite decided whether to run again for public office. At a time when the public-relations man seemed to be running everything from Washington to Seventh Avenue, the rumors said that Lindsay was considering turning public-relations man. He would join with a prominent merchant and a financial man and the three of them would compete to attract the lushest accounts in politics, business, fashion and finance. What could be a more natural image-making machine than a combination of Gracie Mansion, Fifth Avenue and Wall Street? The rumors were, of course, denied on all fronts, and the intriguing idea never came to pass.

*Fly Me, I'm Maurice.* National Airlines, after pushing its offensive TV commercial, "Fly Me, I'm Adele. . . Fly Me, I'm Betty," with pretty stewardesses smiling and inviting the viewer to fly National to Florida, temporarily shifted the "Fly Me" theme from girls to the pleasures of the DC-10 and then back again. But not before Women's Lib groups picketed National's New York office to protest the dirty connotation. And then the Gay Liberation Front, a homosexual organization, entered the situation. It demanded equal consideration—that National name some of its airplanes after men.

*Ohhh, the Timing, the Timing.* In the metropolitan New York area, televiewers were treated to a singular lack of communications sensitivity. After a news announcement reporting the surprising, almost two-for-one vote in a state referendum defeating a proposed $2.5 billion transportation bond issue, three commercials—of which two were consecutive—offered what was hardly in keeping with the dramatic expression of public impatience. The first commercial presented the new Disney World in Orlando, Florida, as "the world where dreams come true." The second, sponsored by General Tire, stressed "the need for reliable tires to track down the Abominable Snowman." And the third was a Getty plug for its premium gas which filled more slowly than "Theirs" because "Getty has more premium to give."

*Not Dishonest, Just Anti-the Unpleasant.* "The public-relations man and the advertising man are no more honest or dishonest than our society—they reflect the ethics that prevail in it," said Henry C. Rogers, chairman of Rogers, Cowan & Brenner, of Beverly Hills and New York, the largest public-relations agency in the entertainment field. "Basically, the chief executive officer isn't dishonest—he just turns his head away from what is unpleasant."

The communications business, Rogers claimed, has been largely cleaned up. "It's more ethical today because it's being forced to become ethical by people like Ralph Nader and the government agencies such as the Federal Trade Commission and the Food and Drug Administration. These have had a tremendous, upbeat effect on our society because they have made us aware of how corrupt our society has been.

"But the nature of man is basically corrupt and dishonest and as long as we have forces compelling us to be ethical and honest, as long as we have someone looking over our shoulder, we will be. But as soon as that stops, we will go right back to where we were."

In the year and a half in which I interviewed many people in both the advertising and public-relations fields, I often heard that refrain. The practitioners, the professionals, look you straight in the eye and insist that they cannot be blamed and should not be called to account for their own actions. Only society can be indicted. There, they point accusingly, is the real culprit.

Is it? It is a claim that will be explored in detail in this book. My aim will be to present all sides of the argument of persuasion vs. manipulation, deception vs. naive acceptance. The foregoing dozen illustrations, anecdotes and interviews-in-brief represent a sprinkling of subjects which will be expanded upon and discussed in subsequent chapters. The result, I hope, will allow you to come to your own conclusions.

That is, if you can avoid the temptation to play the game of self- and mutual deception with everyone else in order to seem what you are not.

# 2.

## The Game of
## Deception
## That *You* Play

*Can you resist the temptation to play the game of
deception?* I doubt that you can—nor can I. All of us are
so locked into a hypoed society where competition for
status and even dominance is hung on a many-pronged
set of false criteria—like a comb with all the teeth bent
the wrong way—that is difficult, almost impossible, not
to play the game. The alternative, not to play it, will
make you come on as a sort of freak—a misfit, an eccen-
tric, an antisocial type. Or at least make you seem to be
one of those types to a degree that will provoke enough

discomfort for you so that you will be constantly tested, jabbed and pushed by everyone else who is playing the deception game.

Let's try a typical morning. We'll skim it here, hitting only the high spots, because later on we'll retrace it in detail in connection with your relations on the job, with your boss, friends, family.

It is 7:00 A.M., or 8:00, or 9:00, or whenever your alarm brings you back to life.

You sit up on the edge of your bed, forgetting for the moment either your wife or your husband (either sex is equally delusive) breathing regularly or awake on the bed beside you. You don't say good morning, or, if you do, it is muttered angrily or sleepily. *You* have gotten up. He or she hasn't, still wrapped in a cataleptic state, partly or entirely, the lucky so-and-so. Why? you ask yourself irritably.

Sitting there, you grimace as you think of your job. You've got to get to it, to put on the garb of deception that is needed there, and in those first waking moments even the best job seems a chore, burdensome, a constant grating against your sensitive nature. But do you say, "Another day, another lousy dollar," or some variation thereof? Probably not. You withhold that confidence, but should your spouse be alert and nasty enough to ask in muffled tones from the secure warmth of the bed, "Another day, another lousy dollar, dear?" chances are you will probably mumble something indiscernible in reply. Who wants to seem such a boor at that early hour?

(Incidentally, the word "seem" is a key word in the game of deception. Depending upon the degree of your deceiving nature, the question of how you "seem" to others, both those with whom you are intimate and those with whom you are not, will trouble you all the days of your life. This goes well beyond the need to observe the amenities, the propriety that society demands of you as one of its responsible components. What I am suggesting here is that the game that you and I are constantly playing is nothing less than a conscious and perhaps subconscious reluctance to let anyone else see us as we really are. Animals don't have that problem. We do.)

In the kitchen, you eat without much pleasure but give your wife the impression that everything is fine by careful pressure of your lips, an impression of enjoying the bitter coffee by taking a good swallow and seeming to savor it. The toast or the English muffin is hard, hurts your lips, pierces your tender gums perhaps, but probably you don't acknowledge that. The cereal may be lumpy, cold, oversweet or too sour, or whatever. If you mention it, you immediately regret it. Why should this day be any different from any other? you wonder in a flash of masochism.

The children, if they are up, speak to you mechanically, as does your wife. And you listen with only a portion of your mind, the major area of its exercise being devoted to a fretful anticipation of the day ahead. "Are you listening?" one of your loved ones might ask. Furiously, you nod. "Of course—I may look [seem] not to be listening, but I am, believe me," you reply, thinking you big liar, you. Even the hurt in your wife's eye, or the kids', doesn't quite reach you. But you do listen, concentrating, one might say, outwardly.

And so it goes until you leave your home, your castle. As you shave, you tell your reflection that the sideburns are not really too long, the flashes of silver among them are just the fluorescent light bouncing back, the thickening of the jowls only the exaggeration of the pose. You dress, and depending upon your particular hangup, you convince yourself that the suit is not really too young for you, with its wide lapels and side vents, or that the thin-lapel, center-vent model isn't too old. There is in you a core of a swinger—darn it all, who knows that better than you? But you ask yourself: When did you last swing? No matter—the inquirer is not persistent.

On the highway, or in a train, subway or bus, you draw a deep breath, but the frown is fixed. The day's pressures have begun, really just a resumption of where they left off yesterday. You curse at the car that edges a bit too close on the freeway, but when the big, rough-looking guy with the baseball cap opens his window and demands, "What the hell'd you say?" you just shake your head. Or on the Amtrak, you dust off the scuff on your pants leg that the slob next to you put there with his big foot. He stares at you in irritation that you should so recognize his lack of consideration. Do you remind him, "Can't you be more careful there?" Does he say, "Sorry about that." No in either case, probably.

Your car now approaches the toll booth, or a narrowing in the multilane highway, an opportunity for you to show some consideration yourself. Do you? Although you despise it in others, you race the motor and slide ahead of cars that were ahead of you, barely avoiding a collision, but by baring your teeth you are in. You have asserted yourself, as you should, rather than let those other bastards best you. After all, you do want the privilege of dropping your coins in first, don't you?

On the bus or the subway, it is not essentially different. You grab a seat and occupy it for the duration, ignoring the old, the pregnant, the ill and the very young. What? You didn't? Instead you surrender it to someone else and now you stand there, noble for the moment but conscious of the accusing eyes of all the others who didn't get up as you did. You are convinced that they are wondering about you. Is he a freak, a do-gooder, a bleeding heart? Just what the hell kind of a person gives up a seat nowadays? The proof of the question may well be in the fact, you tell yourself regretfully, that the recipient of your largess didn't even say thanks but instead fixed a questioning gaze on you as if to ask, "What made you wait so long, buster?"

And then, on the way if you're on the highway you become conscious of either billboards or signs just off the service road; or if you're on the bus or subway, of the interior car cards. You scan them; they haven't changed much in the last few days, and in all probability you feel a stirring of resentment. Don't they know that at 8:00, 9:00, or 10:00 A.M., the last thing you want to face is a sales pitch for toothpaste, gas, a home loan, mouthwash or insurance? So when is the best time? Never, as far as you're concerned, but you know that this is a disloyal thought for any American to think, much less say. The American economy rolls on a wide tread of hucksterism, everyone is selling something good, bad or indifferent, and so you turn an innocent, open face to the pitch, patriotically so to speak, although it is not reaching you as of now and you promise yourself it never will.

In the building, the elevator starter, or the operator himself, or the security guard, gives you a bright, cheery good morning. You are somewhat taken aback by the enthusiasm, and, as you decide on a reply, the thought crosses your consciousness that it isn't too far to Christmas or New Year's and that gifts are on his mind. So you may or may not purse your lips and reply in a noncommittal way. Everybody seems to have their hands out, whether they deserve it or not (don't they get a salary?), you tell yourself, making an exception of yourself, of course. Of course.

And so, you open the door of Valhalla, the place you work. It hasn't changed much since yesterday or over the weekend, and it is as drab, as mundane as ever. Or as antiseptically modern as ever, devoid of warmth and of the inviting atmosphere that leads to wholesome creativeness. Soon, in a matter of moments, you will face the man or woman you work for, or the people who work for you, and already you are bracing yourself with the frozen smile of cheerfulness and anticipation that you believe he, she or they expect of you.

By that early hour of the day, you have already been a hypocrite at least a dozen times, although you will probably never acknowledge it. It isn't, of course, that you meant to be such a reprehensible character but that it is just hard for you to escape from being a victim of yourself and your circumstances. That you easily, maybe even justifiably, tell yourself, should you make such an appraisal of your behavior that morning, which is, of course, very unlikely.

At any rate, you step through the transom and you are there, your place of business, the base from which you pursue your career, and a new, perhaps the most peculiar phase of the game of delusion begins.

THE FOISTING OF AN
ILLUSION, OR, RELATIONS
WITH YOUR BOSS

If the word "seem" is the key one in the game, then "illusion" is the integral one in your relations with your superior on the job. As you take your desk, your bench, your seat or your stool, or merely check in before leaving for the field, you catch your first morning glimpse of him and it hits you how naturally responsibility leads to stature. A short, fat man with a bald head, for example, becomes with a title Romanized, stern, and distinguished, the lack of hair adding rather than detracting because the face and the pate are all one now, a sort of shining avenue of authority. Or a tall, skinny, nervous guy who, with the designation of responsibility, turns lean, whiplike, a wolfhound of brainpower, decisiveness and action.

And you? You are, depending on your quotient of ambition and drive, just the right associate for him. You know you aren't, of course, but you have determined down deep in your gut that you will give that appearance, that illusion. At the first chance, your greeting is warm, confident, friendly, although you would rather ask him what happened to your last few requests such as for a raise, a better desk, more interesting assignment, the vacation dates you wanted rather than what could be fitted into the schedule. His reply gives you the tip to his mood, to his attitude about you. Perfunctory, it dismays you; enthusiastic, it inspires you; noncommittal, it leaves you in your usual state of uncertainty.

It will apparently be one of those days.

It might well go like this. Passing by your desk a few times, his eyes on some more distant objective, he doesn't acknowledge your presence and the worry flashes through you as you try to recall whether and where he has found you lacking, whether you forgot to do something. Then, sans warning, there he is at your side, saying, "Good morning, Bill. Where are we on the Wheeling business?" Or some other unfinished business that may interest him. And then:

"Hi, George," you reply. "The Wheeling thing is all taken care of. No problem." You exude a confidence you probably don't feel, hoping he won't press for details, although you are reasonably certain you can fake it if he does.

But you're lucky—as usual. He doesn't press it. He relaxes a bit at your desk, sitting on the edge or leaning on it. "What else is cooking at your end, Bill?" he asks easily.

The friendliness is evident and you respond warmly with the exercise of the illusion. "Oh, I've been meaning to talk to you about some ideas I have to develop some new business—"

"Oh? Good. Like what?"

"Well, I was wondering if we couldn't begin a new canvassing program out in the new areas on the north side of the river. There's been some important changes in the population mix out there. And then, I happened to be looking through the real-estate section of the Sunday paper and I see a lot of ads for new homes down at the state line. Both these two things might open up some real opportunities for us."

He nods solemnly, studying you. Does he know that

the ideas are coming straight at him from the first flush of your illusive nature, your first, off-the-top layer of imagination? "Sounds good," he says, vaguely, straightening up. "Why don't you"—he pauses—"drop me a memo?" He walks away and you wonder about illusion, yours and his. Who is pushing whose most?

That, it becomes clear, is the way it is with illusion, because for most of the rest of the day your relationship flounders in a bed of uncertainty. It is hardly eased by the events of the day, each one wrinkling the boss's face (not a sensitive one but prone to reflect the pains of the unexpected), followed by occasional, desperate glances around the staff as if to single out some particular laggard or perhaps hypocrite whose ability to cast an illusion is not among the best.

Maybe it is his unique ability to worm through his day without making a single major decision that causes you to suspect that your boss knows more about the deception game than you ever will. The knowledge comes upon you directly and indirectly:

You pass by his desk and your shell-like elephant ears overhear his secretary telling him that a decision on a certain matter has yet to be made. He nods vaguely while continuing to shuffle papers. "Get me Silvestri in statistical," he tells her, and you can see by her expression that he has sidestepped the issue.

Then, too, you present a decision for him to make—a request for your field trip of more than usual distance, or a jurisdictional problem, of some sort. He frowns meaningfully, promising to resolve it, but you know he means instead to worry it into a state of indecision. A minor matter being harassed into a major one because of irresolution. They always said this about him—he could make more decisions without making any than any ten guys in the place. All he did was to let the need grow old and then disappear because of lack of food and oxygen. A typical, successful, corporate executive passing through life without creating any flaps, even ripples.

What does all this do to you, the illusion caster? You, of course, never, never let your true feelings show—that's disastrous. Instead of saying, "Can't you ever make a decision, you boob?" you say, too kindly, "No hurry, of course, let me know when you decide." And you walk away with the bright light of energy and esprit in your eye that you know he wants to see there. Why let the bastard see anything else?

What would happen, you can't help asking yourself, if people in business would communicate truthfully, candidly, instead of preserving a mutual illusion? Chaos, disorganization, total disarray, a virtual halt in the flow of progress? Probably. Or would it be a mutual respect, a more pragmatic grappling with issues, some new progress and new ideas? It's hard to know which because we've never tried it.

They do, here and there. In some corporate situations there is a man-to-man relationship where intellectual honesty and real candor create a wonderful working environment. It endures, brightening the lives of the people involved and the fortunes of the company they work for—until someone else in a key spot sees it as the antithesis of illusion and pushes the panic button, returning the situation to the usual forms of deception.

DANGLING THE BAUBLE,
OR, RELATIONS WITH
YOUR EMPLOYEES

Let's say now you're it, the
boss. You've got quite a parcel of problems, but that's
why they pay you the $75,000 a year, or should. But your
biggest problem, not surprisingly, is that of motivating
people, a tough matter because in this day of strong
unionism, a shortage of skilled workers and general corporate paternalism, the whole situation is tantamount
with making do, to suffer with them "for they are our
children," as one supervisor put it, studying his staff,
tears of frustration welling in his eyes.

So, the implicit word in your relationship with those
who work for you must be "promise," the assurance that
if they put out for you, you will naturally put out for
them. This means, in turn, job security, raises and advancement, plus that essential ingredient in any super-
visor-employee relationship, fringe benefits. This
means a better desk, chair, newer equipment, days off
and other mundane stuff, but privileges, nevertheless.
So, in your dealings with your people, you dangle the
bauble, building, you hope, a firm foundation for good
employee motivation.

"You know, Bill," you tell one of your troublemakers
whose smoothness never really fooled you, "how the
company recognizes performance. It's got its eye on the
guys on the ball."

True enough, but you know well by now that quite

often while the bauble is dangled, it frequently remains out of reach even for the performers. How well you know, for example, that company policy is to fit only square pegs into square holes. What, try a round peg in a square hole? It's unheard of.

But, while you are aware that there is always the hope for an exception to the practice, you are probably a decent enough guy to admit to yourself that this is unlikely. Of course, should you personally push for the exception, it just might come about. But why should you take the risk? When was the last time you did?

If any of this flashes through you as you wear the even-featured, somewhat ennobled but firm expression of authority, you don't tell your employees. Collectively or individually, they are told in so many words that hard work, diligence and application will inevitably pay off. And it does, more than occasionally; but more often it doesn't, extraneous circumstances standing in its way.

And you know those extraneous elements well—hidebound tradition, prejudice, company need, negligence, the demand of other matters, insensitivity and so on.

And so the staff plods on, slowly, if ever, getting the picture, and your motivation to engender motivation flounders. Yet, you, too, are trapped in the game of deception in which dangling the bauble is an integral move. Why? Because, to be utterly frank, the bauble is being dangled at you, too, by your own superiors, and you are just as prone as those who work for you to be hypnotized by it as you vainly reach for it and perhaps never really get it in your grasp. Quid pro quo? I leave the answer to you.

PRESERVING STATUS,
OR, RELATIONS WITH
YOUR FRIENDS

Comes the coffee break or lunch or any other situation that takes you out of your job milieu for a spell and you are justifiably happy about it. Whoever invented the coffee break, or more important the noon hour, had to know intimately the thousand tiny moments of frustration, fatigue and resentment that accumulate during only a few hours on the job and which so badly need relief.

So you sip, drink, eat with your coworkers or friends. Do you drop the attempt at illusion? No, it seems not, not much anyway. Of course, you relax a bit, you drop your guard a trifle—but only a trifle. The visor in the helmet remains up. You're skeptical. Be on guard with your colleagues, especially your pals. All right, let's try a few typical bits of conversation:

"Hi, Bill," says your friend, "think you'll get that promotion?"

"Who, me?" you ask incredulously. "Not a chance." (But you know darned well you hope and think you will.)

"Would you be disappointed if you don't?" your friend pursues.

"Hell, no," you reply airily. "Why should I?" (But you know, you do know that not getting it will just about cripple you.)

"You think Gene might get it?" he asks.

The Argument

"He'd be a good choice," you say. (He would? You know he'd be terrible, not half as good as you. What is he after all but a show-off?)

OR

"What do you think about the new company crackdown on lateness and excessive absenteeism?" wonders your friend and coworker.

"Kind of rough, if you ask me," you reply.

"Why the hell don't they concentrate more on improving conditions?" he says.

You shrug. (But secretly you're happy about the crackdown. Why should you be so diligent and prompt when everyone else is goofing off?)

"Wonder what started it?" he asks.

"I don't know," you answer, truthfully for once. (Although in your inside self, you're glad—things have been getting too sloppy lately and you feel a bit of well-deserved vindication in it all, but you certainly won't say so.)

Of course, I grant you that you may act a bit more honest in either of these two situations, but the question is, How much more? The maintenance of status between contemporaries and peers is one of the big influences in human relationships and nowhere more so than in that illusion-prone hotbox, the place you work. I am referring to status both professional and personal, and I suggest that it is the moving factor in your relationship with others. And as far as the scene where you spend two-thirds of your waking hours directly or indirectly, I am almost willing to forego any other major stimuli for the way you—and I—behave.

© 29

And in order to achieve and maintain status, you simply resort to a constant game of illusion. Here are a few hypothetical examples:

If a friend or fellow employee asks you how you're making it on the job, do you reply: (1) Fine (2) Good (3) Fair (4) Poor (5) Unsure. Once you select the answer, then ask yourself why you chose it. Was it (1) True (2) Only partly true (3) An outright lie (4) You really don't know, so you had to cover up (5) Why should you expose a problem, anyway? (6) Would it help to reply otherwise? (7) If not any of these, then——?

If a fellow employee asks you if you intend to apply for a transfer to a job listed on the bulletin board, do you reply (1) Yes (2) No (3) Maybe (4) I don't really know (5) Should I? Regardless of your reply, it is worth examining again why you made it. The reply is a direct signal to your own status, a tip to your real feelings, hence a challenge to how you want to look in the eyes of others. Is that so important? As a question, that's one of the big ones.

It's not much different with your friends. The degree to which you want to open up with them depends on how close you are to them. But even within that freedom, your basic sense of insecurity just won't permit you to go so far that your status will falter in their eyes.

Let's go one step further and probably be accused of a completely antisocial attitude. The trouble with friends, either business or social in nature, and even good ones, I am compelled to tell you, is that you can never fully rely on them either to understand you or to remain loyal, not to use such an old-fashioned word as steadfast. In today's harsh, tight world, the social and emotional pressures that impinge on the individual make this even more true than in the past. Thus, you tend to keep your innermost feelings and convictions to yourself for fear—let's face it—that you will be handed over to the enemy, betrayed, and left to their resources, treacherous as they may be.

A HOME ISN'T A CAVE,
OR, RELATIONS WITH
YOUR FAMILY

Your home is your refuge against the world, your cave where no marauding animals can enter, and the people in it are not only your flesh and blood but your companions against the coldness, cruelty, hypocrisy and evils of the world. Together —you hope—your family unit means the ramparts of decency and truth.

Or so it seems. . . .

It is, in fact, not so at all.

Over the centuries, few elements in life have been so favored, so eulogized, so pictured in warm, humble tones as the home. "There is no place more delightful than home," observed a Greek poet thousands of years ago. "A man travels the world over in search of what he needs, and returns home to find it," philosophized George Moore. "It takes a heap o' livin t' make a house a home," said Edgar A. Guest. But Ogden Nash may have been closer to the mark. "Home is heaven and orgies are vile," he wrote, "but I like orgies once in a while."

© 31

The brutal but inescapable fact is that home and family are a dictatorial unit, going the way of a dominant parent or willful offspring or a combination of both. The family's behavior, in other words, is attuned to the illusion that the dominating factor wishes to create, whether it is perfection, obedience, indolence, affluence, penuriousness, culture, nonculture or what not.

If home is the catalytic factor in society, the honey cell in the beehive of our daily activity, it also revolves on a turret spun by its strongest member, who enforces a totalitarian or more subtly arbitrary pressure on all within it. This entails a particular illusion in the home to which all family members adhere, and each family differs in this respect from any other. No two are alike.

Now I don't mean to frighten you. I don't mean to twist your deep feeling that your home is a warm cave which keeps out the foragers into something resembling a jail. It is much more casual, more subtle than that. My contention is that almost every home reflects in many obvious and hidden ways the influence and demands of its most vibrant or dramatic personality. Thus, it casts, it is redolent with and vibrates with, Momism, Popism, the New Youth or whatever is the personality thrust of the most dominant member. And that thrust, that demand, is usually of a pervasive enough nature to compel everyone to bend, swing, to give in to it.

This is really not so startling. It is only a natural evolution from the protectionism that the Neanderthal man felt stirring in his breast as he regarded his mate and the suckling child she held. As he saw the hot, hungry eyes of his shrunken world glaring at him, he laid down certain rules for the security of his cave, rules that changed as time did. But in their insistence on obedience, they became the standard behavior in the family unit, with necessary variations, for centuries forward.

But the environment of the home, its format, its overtones, even its influence on its more impressible residents do not represent rules or standard behavior anymore as much as an artificial microsociety, in effect, a set of illusions manipulated for the sake of perpetuation of a personality who insists that a practical philosophy, a concept of life, even a favorite idea be acted out by his or her family.

So now you, having foisted an illusion, dangled a bauble or fought to have your status unchanged, all by withholding your real self, head home to your cave world, forgetting or maybe just not knowing that it is hardly that. It, too, is an exercise in illusion.

You walk into your living room and your bride of a year, or a decade or two, confronts you, and you feel it emanating from her or she from you or both. Possessiveness, domination, infatuation, indifference, frigidity, remoteness, whatever. In a hundred ways from that moment, the evening and night carry the evocations of that trait or traits that throb between you. These build an emotional framework for all those hours and days that will come ahead.

And so it is with your relations with your children: you or they falling reluctantly into line with the moving personality's ability to convince and command.

Who triggers the home illusion? And why? This is the area of the psychiatrist and psychotherapist, and the matter will be probed into in some detail in the two chapters that follow.

But at this stage it really doesn't matter who triggers the home illusion. Each family unit and home represents the object of such a manipulation of sight, sound and thought, a mosaic of illusion that every home knows only too well. It is probably the most important gambit in the game of deception, because our society reflects the behavior of its basic components.

Thus, the evening goes and the night, too, and your morning begins again. A full circle in the game of personal and mutual deception has been completed. Only in your sleeping hours, apparently, does it stop. But then, who knows what intragame intricacies your subconscious has performed while you slept?

Can you resist the temptation to play the game of deception? The more proper question is, Can you avoid it?

Here's why.

# 3.

## The
## Double-Bind
## and the Deficits

IT MAY COME as a rude shock, but you are a major, willing contributor to the deceptions that others work on you. Deep in your psychological and emotional makeup lurks some built-in deception orifices. These are traits, frustrations, gaps, weaknesses which make you an easy mark for the manipulators of values through false messages and deceptive communications. They even allow friends and members of your own family to take advantage of you.

Those traits of yours permit the game of "double-bind" to be played to confuse you and to make you the victim of opposing or contradictory messages.

© 35

Other traits, mostly representing frustrations, represent "deficits" which enable others to twist your motives and actions.

So deeply entrenched are these traits, psychiatrists say, that when they are brought into play because of someone else's deceptive act, we ourselves are not aware that we are being victimized.

First, the double-bind . . .

The words are warm, the voice is friendly but the eyes are ice cold.

"That's fine, thank you," the words assure smoothly in an employer-employee situation. Yet, the steel gray of the eyes, the stiffness of the jowls, the set of the jaw transmit just the opposite. They say, silently but eloquently, "Nothing that you can do, no matter how good it is, will ever satisfy me."

Or, in a strained marital situation, it is the tone of the voice that belies the soothing words. The utterance is, "It's all right, dear," but the tone says, "You damn bitch . . ."

Or, an overanxious mother tells an anxious fifteen-year-old girl, "You can't go out with boys . . . you're too young . . . you don't know enough about boys yet . . . you have to stay indoors . . . go but be back by nine thirty . . . don't forget that you're only fifteen. . . ."

If this sort of thing sounds familiar to you, it isn't surprising. It is the highly prevalent form of communication between people nowadays which might even be called noncommunication. But, more accurately, it is a form of communication that involves the sending out of two contradictory messages at the same time, either both verbal or one verbal and the other implied.

The recipient of the messages, faced by what are clearly opposite meanings, isn't sure and doesn't know which to believe and hence is confused which to follow.

He is, as a result, hung up in his reaction, bound not by one but by two messages and opposing ones at that. Thus, he is in a "double-bind."

It happens all the time. And it involves most people.

The dual-message principle was first discovered about twenty years ago by a team of innovative sociologists and psychotherapists studying the problems of family dissensions in a California mental hospital. Experimenting with psychologically troubled patients, they found that more than one target patient would probably never get well because he wasn't mentally or emotionally self-sufficient. Unable to live a normal, balanced life of his own in contemporary society, his involvement—and "bind" with his own family—permitted him to preserve a semblance of normality in ordinary situations. But since he was not an adequate "unit" by himself, he apparently could exist only when "protected" by the umbrella of his own family.

Probing the intricate fabric that lay underneath this type of situation, the study team decided to work with entire families, no longer isolating the troubled patient himself but probing the internal behavior of the family. The result was the perception of some new elements in the area of personal communications. They began to see that much family behavior responded to attitudes bearing two different kinds of messages, both simultaneous and often contrary.

While at first it seemed to involve primarily an effect on children, the investigation developed a similar effect on adults. Hanging on an obligation between people, whether in a family, other social or economic situation, the conveyance of distinctly different attitudes by the very same person or persons produced a disturbing and confusing effect. If the facial expression can say one thing and the voice another, if the words convey at one and the same time a request and an exhortation to do just the reverse, if someone smiles at you but says the most hostile, one-upmanship things, how do you react? How can you react?

Hence the double-bind.

The theory proved to be one of the first real breakthroughs in psychiatry vis-à-vis communications between people.

But why the double-bind compulsion? Why do people behave in that disturbing way when life would be simpler, more honest and more wholesome if they would just be straight with one another, considerate and decent? This question, unfortunately, could easily be taken as naive, ingenuous; for people are hardly simple, straight, considerate.

When the question was put to some psychiatrists who are close to the problems of human communications, the basis for the double-bind principle elicited this reason why people—you and I—behave and talk to one another in a covert and cover-up manner:

There is a sharp conflict within each of us between our behavior to the "outside" world and what we on the "inside" of ourselves feel, or want or don't want. As a well-known New York psychiatrist put it:

> All of us cater to the so-called "outside world." We have a whole series of obligations, mannerisms and attitudes

which we have learned are acceptable to the outside world. You don't go up to your boss and call him a "son-of-a-bitch." Why not? You may sometimes feel that he is one but you just don't do it. You complicate this single instance by 10,000, perhaps 100,000 kinds of things. . . . You have a certain attitude in a supermarket, at a cocktail party, in the office. Suppose you were invited to a White House party; you would put on a particular kind of manners, but if you were invited to play cards with friends, you would put on a different kind of manners, wouldn't you? The point is that you would gauge your kind of response to the outside situation—and there are all manner of sets of responses which are on tap for a reasonably intelligent, reasonably adjusted person. You don't have to think about them, either. If you were invited to the Rockefeller's for dinner, you wouldn't behave as though you were invited to the neighbor's for dinner. Somehow, all your total experience would involve you in a sense that these people are fantastically rich and somehow have powers that you don't have by virtue of this wealth, and therefore your whole manner, your speech, would be quite different from dining with neighbors or friends. But when you come into contact with your peers, you have another set of values and attitudes. In other words, we all have our set behavior as to how to respond to a particular situation and that's the "outside." You learn the values and attitudes of the various ingredients of your environment and you are aware of them, you accept them and accede to them, even though your accession to these values may be at a particular moment at absolute odds with what you want to do and to be.

According to this therapist, if a child, for example, knows that when it spills a glass of water, it will be smacked on the hand or even face, the child really learns what it is supposed to do or not do. And we learn such things from ages of a few months, maybe even earlier, developing some semblance of attitude perhaps prenatally. The psychiatrist adds: "But we very soon in the first few years of our lives begin to distinguish between what is demanded on the outside—everything on the outside, father, mother, nurse, table, everything— and what we on the inside of ourselves feel or want. This is a sort of dividing line that becomes more and more complex as the child grows into an adult."

Where does all this lead? And how is the conflict between outside attitudes and inner compulsions resolved? For the answer, you have to go to the barnyard —literally—because that is where Konrad Lorenz, the Austrian ethologist, and others who joined him, discovered that animals were communicating in a very specific way. This communication, they perceived, had a practical purpose—to substitute a set of behavior patterns for direct acts of violence.

To kill—or to confront in terms of direct violence or affirmative resolution—is what psychologists call "contra-adaptative." Thus, if two animals (people) of the same species kill (compete violently with) each other because of rivalry over a female of the species (or position in a job), they are simply reducing their capacity to adapt to their environment.

But, as the herd instinct grew and matured among animals, as man learned to curb his baser passions for sake of communal living, each developed the substitution of a set of physical behavior patterns for the actual intent of committing violence. The result is that each goes through a series of acted-out actions which control, repress and at the same time give some satisfaction to his needs.

For example, your behavior to your boss is a cover-up for your real feeling, but acted-out it gives the message, "You see, boss, I'm really not angry with you or envious of you. I really want to follow your leadership, I think it's just great. . . . And I really don't want you to feel that I have any feelings in my gut other than what my behavior is showing you."

Part of this cover-up in communications is deliberate, part of it is learned; part of it is subconscious and part of it is highly conscious. But a lot of it is automatic or what the psychiatrists call "deeply internalized."

So that is the gambit. As in chess, so it is in life— tricks, feints, ploys by which to achieve goals other than by direct means. Or, put another way, controls which you in your own milieu develop to guard against the "contra-adaptation" that direct expression of your innermost desires would create and, in principle if not in effect, wipe out the species.

The double-bind principle is merely the end result of the duality that lurks deeply in everyone, human or animal. You could call it the acted-out action in action.

Of course, it's axiomatic that people sending out double-bind messages often strive for at least superficial rapport. But the result is no less disturbing or disconcerting to the recipient of the messages. Even some of the most classical double-binds show this: "When did you stop beating your wife?" "You look tired, did you work hard today?" "I'm not hungry, honey, I ate in a good restaurant today." "Bill—how busy are you?—I'd like you to do something right away." "Officer, I'm sorry to interrupt you [in your siesta] but which way is Main Street?"

All in all, the double-bind is an important component

in the game of deception, the game of deluding communications process in which everyone is engaged. It could almost be the very game of deception itself, except that there's more to it, especially when it comes to such important matters as family and sex.

And that brings us to the "deficit."

Probably no one ever told you but it's there just the same. You have a deficit, a kind of hole in your psychic stomach, an empty place in your mental and emotional viscera that you want to fill up.

It's a hunger for something that you missed on the way to maturity or happiness because you never experienced it. But your instinct wants it, even craves it, and so you walk around for years with it, consciously or usually subconsciously aware of it. It affects your behavior and influences the way you communicate with others, sometimes moderately, sometimes seriously. Because of it, you are simply not complete, either in your ability to communicate or, sad to say, as a human being.

That's what the psychiatrists say.

"None of us lives in perfect families, and in most that I have had anything to do with, something gets left out of one or more members and it is something that they simply cannot help," observed Sophie Linden, a skilled psychotherapist who practices in New York and London.

Parents quickly determine their hopes for a child, she explained, and what they hope and expect is conveyed to the child in ways which may be indirect or "double-bound." These adults develop great expectations and great fervor for their hopes over the years and almost from the child's birth. In order to bow to, or to achieve, these expectations, the young man or woman may miss a lot of the blowups that adolescents have, or miss some of the sports and games, "running around, going crazy, all part of the roughnecking of the adolescent."

And what has been missed represents a "deficit," a missing piece in the whole pattern of growing up.

"The person who evolves equally on every level all the time," said Mrs. Linden, "is very rare. Most of us evolve sufficiently on every level to become fairly adequate, functioning mature people. But what we miss in one area or another remains a deficit, a hankering, a lost piece in a crossword puzzle or a missing piece in the whole set of evolution."

In some people, the missing parts are so many that they will never evolve as completely happy people at all. Some will become extremely successful professionally, intellectually, and yet, noted Mrs. Linden, occasionally a bank president at the age of fifty-five commits suicide. Why?

"It's a puzzle, it seems almost ridiculous, because such a man seemed to have everything going for him, and yet something in his personal evolution was missing," she said. "Maybe he was just a lousy lover, maybe he never felt comfortable socially, never knocked around as a boy, never had sneaked behind a fence and smoked cigarettes like a lot of kids, maybe he just never tried out the bad things and so he had a continuous hankering to do something of that kind."

These days, young people appear to be sensitive to the need to avoid "deficits," or, at least, conscious of the need to have a broad variety of experiences. "If they overspecialize in academic superiority," she pointed out, "they think they're going to miss something, the horsing around, the girls or the boys, the sex or the give-and-take experience of the opposite sex, the parties, the smoking, the pot, the drinking. I don't just mean the men; the girls, too, miss a lot of such things but they seem to be expressing themselves through Women's Lib, all the things that young men can do but that they cannot do, or haven't done up till now."

The deficit problem comes to the surface in many marriages.

## A Typical Case History

A young man between the ages of twenty-two and twenty-eight decides it is time he got married. He is, let's say, really tops professionally or intellectually but what he is hankering for is something that he has been missing all his life, a particular kind of freedom. He wants to be a hippie, or to lead that kind of life for a while. But he's always been too busy and always told himself, "If I go off that way, God help me, I'll never get back to getting top grades in my tests." But, he finally decides that he will seek a compromise. If he can't be a hippie—and it probably isn't in him to go that far, anyway—at least he can become a swinger. Or, maybe, he can find a swinging kind of girl, someone who looks sexy and is attractive. He feels instinctively that if he meets and marries such a girl, she can bring him into a world of dissipation or freedom or wildness that he has missed all his life.

"Now, let's take the swinger," said the psychiatrist. "She's that, all right, but perhaps she is also a girl who really wanted to be somebody, or had a tremendous need to go to college, to become a professional person, and maybe she even had a high IQ naturally but it couldn't be satisfied.

"So the two marry and they believe that, golly, he (or she) is going to give me what I need. Each has an outer camouflage, which appears to say that 'I can give this to you.' After the marriage, each begins to start taking from the other person what they think they bargained for, for their marriage really was a sort of emotional contract. He thinks, 'I've been sort of isolated all my life, more or less shy of people, but you are a very gregarious and social animal, you're going to fill my life with 10,000 people.' She thinks, 'You're going to acquaint me with the intellectual life, you're going to bring me up to the upper classes.' So now they expect to get the fulfillment of their expectations."

If all this were spelled out in a real contract, it would be reasonable, even legal, to say, "You promised me this, you promised me that." But humans aren't like that and they aren't aware of all their motivations or, for that matter, their deficits. So, now they begin to make demands of an opposite sort of each other and gradually each realizes that you can't fill your deficits from the other person. "You can't fill a hole in your belly except by eating. You can't satisfy a hunger in your life except by actually eating. If you have a fantasy in which you compose successful popular songs, you have to write songs. You can't marry someone who writes songs and feel that you are the one who has done the achieving," said Mrs. Linden.

Many marriages suffer from this lack of understanding, which is really a lack of communication, but, fortunately, most marriages are not entirely like this. "In happy, positive marital relationships," she went on, "each person feels, 'I have grown up, I have matured, I can be a person to you and you can be a person to me and we can talk well together in most areas and honestly and we can be good for each other.'"

But where the relationship depends on a deficit demand, then the marriage goes sour. Each person thinks that the other has done him dirt. "He hasn't lived up to in a sense what he has promised, and the same with her. And so they are always fighting. And they don't really know what they are fighting about. Actually, they're fighting from a sense of justice, they're fighting because they feel guilty, they shouldn't be making these demands in the first place. And all the time what they are really trying to do is to grow up in their own way."

### An Actual Case History

A suburban New York couple was having problems. He was a college graduate who had a science-technology position. But he was a very emotionally deprived guy who had grown up with a stepmother and developed the feeling that no one really wanted him. He married a woman who gave the appearance of being a tough, controlling, managing kind who "indeed does a certain kind of mothering. She runs the household, she orders everyone around, she tells them what to buy, where to go and when."

The husband was unhappy, the children were confused and unhappy, and the woman herself was depressed.

Said Mrs. Linden: "When I began to intervene in this really tormented relationship, I said to the wife, 'You have some needs that you aren't beginning to fulfill.' She had a hankering to drive a car, for example. It would mean status, control of her environment, in a way. So I said to her, 'Apart from everything else, apart from what is going on in your marriage, what are the obstacles that are preventing you from learning to drive? You live, after all, in the suburbs, you'll have a lot more mobility, freedom. . . . I felt without saying so that the problems of communicating, of getting along with her husband and family, stemmed from some deeply rooted deficits. But she had a thousand rationalizations. She was scared stiff of driving a car. Having come from a poor family, it was above the status of her youthful years even to have a car. She just didn't conceive of herself as a person who could manage in this way, although she and her husband could well afford to have an extra car. Well, she became convinced that she could have a car and, more important, learn to drive it, and she did. It didn't cure her neurosis by a longshot but it did move her along."

The wife had another hankering, representing another deficit, and it turned out to be an important one. She had always wanted to play the piano. Urged by the psychiatrist to take lessons, the woman did, and it turned out that she was rather good at it. "It gave her a certain feeling that she had accomplished something but it also made her feel more feminine. She had always associated playing the piano with femininity and graciousness. Since she didn't play the piano, it was one of the things that she felt made her less feminine. But

© 47

filling that deficit was another step along the way for her. . . ."

As Mrs. Linden pointed out, one way of treating people who are in deep conflict maritally is to help them fill their deficits and to show them the demands that each makes on the other that they can't fulfill that way. Only each can fill his or her own deficits.

### Sex—the Combination of the Double-Bind and the Deficits

How much is sex a game of delusion? According to Mrs. Linden, who has specialized in marital relations, "Sex is used to a large extent to prove something, except by those people who are very free sexually."

A man, for example, has to prove that he can satisfy a woman. If he can't, then what's wrong with him? He's not masculine, he is convinced, and so he's a man in a state of deficit in some way.

A woman, on the other hand, feels that if she can't turn on her man, what kind of a female is she?

So both of them start putting on an act, quite unconsciously.

After intercourse, the man will say, "Are you all right, have I given you an orgasm, are you fulfilled?" If she is, he feels good. But they miss the basic point that sex is really for oneself. The woman tells herself, "If you turn me on, and I go wild with you, what better compliment can I pay you? I really don't give a hoot about you, but don't I pay you a tremendous compliment?" She gets gratification only if her response to him is so genuinely turned on that that is the real compliment. So each is acting as though the real prize in the game of sex is to produce a turned-on response in the other. The game is the pretense.

And that pretense is that "I'm good in bed and that is to your benefit as well as a great compliment to you."

Among the middle-aged, it is an old, understood trick of women that they do a lot of pretending, that everything that their husbands do is "a miracle of joy" to them. This, of course, is a lie and a game. A woman, for example, may not feel like sleeping with her man one night but she will probably not say no to him. Because if she says no to him, she is in effect saying, "I'm not a woman and I am insulting you."

Among the youth of today, the situation is different, radically. They want it straight; the pretense is less frequent and simple honesty is more often the case.

But, mostly, even today the relationship between the sexes is what it has been for years. There are those who are "pretty healthy, maybe normal human beings who can tell the truth to each other, who are able to communicate with each other and accept each other as they happen to be or feel at a particular moment. But most people are afraid, the woman feeling, "If I show him that I'm not turned on, he will dislike me or question my love." The man feels exactly the same way, "I've got to prove to my wife that I can have sixty-eight orgasms as fast as you want me to have them."

Added Mrs. Linden, "Well, of course, I'm describing what amounts to cover-ups. The minute people lie to each other in order to pretend that they are more sexual than they actually are, they are playing a game. It is true, of course, that a lot of broken marriages are due to incompatibility, but I think that sexual incompatibility is in itself a symptom of a deeper kind of incompatibility—a deficit incompatibility. It amounts to this, "You can't give me what I lack in myself and I am really angry with you about that. What I expected of you when I married you, you just didn't deliver."

She noted one example that comes up fairly often. Either partner in a marriage may ask silently and later even outwardly: "If I expected you to draw me closer to people, and I happen to be shy and you seem to have a knack with people and then I discover that your apparent knack with people is nothing but phony and that underneath you're really as scared of people as I am, then what the hell good are you to me?"

So much at this point for the double-bind and the deficits.

Each represents an instinctive problem which relates to communication between people and to their reaction toward outward communication beamed at them. How important are these influences on how our society talks to itself? No one really knows for sure, although psychologists and psychiatrists believe that these influences have very definite relevance. But can the advertising and public-relations communities excuse their abuses because of the intrinsic demands, however they reflect internal problems of society's human components?

Only *you* can answer that, and information and facts to help you make that decision easier are the goal of this book.

My own feeling as a writer, as an observer of the scene over the years, is that the professional communicators cannot escape the burdens, the ills, of what they do anymore than pornographers should be tolerated because everyone likes at least a little smut or that criminals shouldn't be punished too severely because we are, after all, a permissive society. My own conviction, admittedly idealistic, is that leadership imposes responsibility, that the public and the consuming market will respond to truth rather than to deception and that deception is the easy way out while truth is the hard way in. But what lasting things, such as loyalty and credibility, both institutional and economic, are earned the easy way?

If you happen to know the answer to that, don't tell the advertising and public-relations men or, more important, their clients. They just may use it against you.

# 4.

## The
## Rebuttal

"THE CONSUMPTION of new ideas, new forms and new styles is so rapid, thanks to mass communications, that the sense of joy they should give is being taken away. People are simply not geared by nature to absorb novelty at that rate. . . ."

"There's a lot of distrust about whether people are saying what they mean or meaning what they say. Some of the consumer discontent with advertisers has been a sort of proxy for a more basic distrust of everybody and everything. It's all very disturbing. . . ."

"All the eloquent communications in the world will not achieve their desired influence if the behaviors they induce do not provide real reward for the consumer. . . . But

I think it is perfectly true that our communicators have become reasonably adroit at finding vulnerability in the human need and in the human psyche. . . ."

It is interesting, if not revealing, to note how a rebuttal often starts out in direct opposition to a premise, but as the opponent explores the depth of his own reasoning, as well as the range of his own rhetoric, he comes close to agreeing with that premise.

I don't say that is precisely what happened in this case. I leave you to judge. But while most people on Madison, Lexington and Third avenues chose to indict society for the ills attributed to their practices, the three highly articulate sources who made the above comments elaborated in depth on why my premise was wrong. In the process, they nevertheless generally tended to confirm that Americans were put upon by the pressures of communications practices, were becoming skeptical and jaded because of excessive promises that were not delivered and were being made the victims of their own vulnerability and weaknesses.

The quotes above were made respectively by Jacques Barzun, an internationally known historian and professor at Columbia University, New York; Nelson Foote, chairman of the sociology department at Hunter College, New York; and Dr. Joseph G. Smith, president of Oxtoby-Smith, Inc., consumer-research consultants, New York.

In separate, prolonged interviews, the three outlined their own positions on the broad communications environment involving society, business, politics and the family. Much of their comment follows in their own words.

## BARZUN: TOO MUCH FOR THE SENSORIUM?

Not long ago, I attended a conference in which a number of powerful minds were concentrating on some aspects of society that contributed to discomfort or despair. The group came to one conclusion—that the consumption of new ideas, new forms and new styles is so rapid, thanks to mass communications, that the sense of joy they should give is being taken away.

For example, someone in the group observed that a new school of thought or a new style in painting, literature and so on lasts nowadays about two months before it becomes old hat. That's bad for people. People are simply not geared by nature to absorb novelty at that rate, nor in the end does it amount to very real novelty because those who are the makers of supposedly new things know that their life span is going to be short.

As a result, they make a great deal of some trivial thing, some tiny detail, instead of working at something for twenty-five years and coming before the public, finding resistance, overcoming it and then for twenty-five years enjoying the reputation, the honor, the emoluments of having done something like Impressionism in nineteenth-century painting.

But now someone starts painting triangles and that's good enough and he switches to squares and ovals and has to produce a lot to make any impact. Everyone says, "How delightful, how wonderful!" But in two months, it's all over and someone else comes on the scene whose name has yet to be learned, whose colors have yet to be memorized and whose stuff then goes on everyone's walls or appears in everyone's magazines.

The rate of consumption and the rate of production are too much for the receptive powers of the ordinary sensorium or the total intake of the personality, mind, senses, memory, eyes and ears.

I think that the excess of stimulation will have a similar effect even on a guinea pig. Stick him too often with a pin or even jab him with a finger and he wants to rebel. He wants to go and live in a commune with a lot of people he knows well. Tired of being battered around not only by individuals in his daily experience but even more profoundly by stimuli in his thoughts and imagination, he hasn't got that much attention to give. It's exhausted daily and not replenished overnight. . . .

It seems to me that we are faced with such a volume, such a multiplicity of sources, channels and so forth that they are getting into one another's way and it is becoming more difficult to be in touch with the information or the knowledge that one wants than it used to be when there were fewer avenues.

Whether you take the scholarly field where journals have multiplied so that no one can keep abreast of them or you take the general, educated man's field or the popular field, in each of them there is a surplus, a superfluity, and the result is confusion, not only among the subjects themselves but what you might call induced confusion in the mind of any individual who doesn't know whether to turn his head to the left or to the right or back or forth to catch it all.

The multiplication of learned journals grows at a

really alarming rate. The scientific ones, not the *Intellectual Digest* but at the more technical level above that, are what I am referring to. In my own field, history, I should read every month, I suppose, something like fifty or sixty journals so that I should be sure not to miss anything. Well, no human being can do that. In the sciences, the abstracts are huge volumes like *Webster's Dictionary* for every year and abstracting is no way to get to the real substance of things.

What's causing this? It may be the great expansion of fields which comes from the greater and greater number of people who are trained to do the competent, average but not inspired job of thousands of specialities. If you go to a person who is really knowledgeable in a field, he will tell you that four-fifths of what is published would be better off not published. It is either repetitious or inflated or leads nowhere or is mere information. It resembles a former dissertation in American history, the recurrent names in 8,000 graveyard inscriptions. Now, who wants to know—? An afternoon in a cemetery is quite enough.

The public suffers from this at the level of general information, news and so on, doesn't know what to believe, reads carelessly, gets some cockeyed idea of what someone has said. And so I think that one of the side effects of improving communications is disimproving the contents of our heads. . . .

And finally, let me refer to the glamour of the Kennedy era, the bright, vibrant image of the beautiful people in the White House. I mean the notion that not only must you have government and a good one but it must be glamorous and popular and interesting for other reasons than the governmental. That's part of the more general thing that affects society today and American society particularly and that is that everything must have all the virtues and not just its own.

Take people who write books. They must not merely write good books but they must themselves do interesting things and be perfectly charming people and have the loveliest wives. A whole lot of nonsensical expectations, in other words, and since the expectations cannot be carried out, then they put on a false front. Whether the photographer makes the author look like a movie star or whether the blurb says that he is something that he is not, the attention is not given to the thing itself but to the packaging.

I am not a believer in the conspiracy theory of anything whatsoever, or a conspiracy to manipulate. Not because people don't conspire and a lot of people think they are clever and they are going to put something over on the rest of us, but because conspiracy takes such talents to work out, people in the conspiracy give it away, people who are opposed to the first lot counterconspire and everything gets mixed up. But there is a lot of manipulation that we are all subjected to and that is the manipulation of norms and forms.

For example, when I'm asked by a radio or TV broadcaster to do something on a subject that I happen to know something about, the first thing that happens is that I'm limited to 15½ or 28½ minutes to do something that will take more or only the allotted time and so there is immediately a distortion through the regular form. And this applies to almost everything that we do. Now, we can't do without norms and forms but I think that in a technological system such as we have today, they're very numerous, absolutely compulsory and yet very destructive.

I encounter similar problems whenever I write an article for a magazine, whether it is a learned journal or a popular, wide-circulation magazine. The first thing that happens is that there are house rules about things to do, no italics or some italics and no quotation marks, we don't put paragraphs in footnotes, all footnotes must be continuous, we don't like hyphens, this word is on our forbidden list because it is indecent or because it is a word that the editor doesn't like or something—

One is always wriggling through a keyhole to get to the supposed public outside and on the claim that the public has made the excuse for this or that. Our readers wouldn't like it—but how do you know if you've never tried it?

Everything is being manufactured instead of being created and everybody is going through contortions over things little and big and once in a while I for one rebel. I say, no, well, there is so much to change, I withdraw the article, let somebody else write for you, not in a spirit of huffiness but because it is tiresome, all this to make sausage out of something that ought to be a chop or a steak and stand for itself. Good or bad, the public likes it, the public dislikes it, who cares?

It all leads me to think that we are too keen about success, we want to please, it's got to be popular, everybody has got to like every bit of it. Nothing human is like that and we'd better stop trying.

FOOTE: NADER, MC LUHAN
AND DISTRUST

I think I have to be a little
critical of your notion that there are misrepresentations
and falsehoods that are propagated with what everybody believes or wants to believe or repeats because he
hears others say it.

P. T. Barnum was at this business a long time ago and
he took some rather inferior artists and made them
worldwide celebrities. He was a genius at publicity and
the evidence seems that he could take mediocre
material and make it look awfully good. So there's nothing new about that. And there have been people like
that, not necessarily as flamboyant or well known but
very successful practitioners of publicity and public relations, for a long, long time. So if you are familiar with
this history, you can't help being a little skeptical about
whether there is something new under the sun. Just
what is new about it? One is that there is a different
degree of concern among certain people in certain businesses about their public relations. While not under direct heavy attack, business in general is now seriously
challenged to a degree that it has not experienced since
the thirties.

Ralph Nader and Marshall McLuhan are the first
names that come up in the critical forefront and who
articulate the great discontent that consumers have today. But I don't consider that either of them has either
fully described or expressed what has been happening.

© 59

Let's talk about McLuhan for the moment. We now have a group of young adults who have been exposed to television since they were born and all of whom suspect that this makes a big difference, but so far as I know no one has successfully explained what the difference is. McLuhan sheds a few flashes of light on it. I think very highly of his *Understanding Media.* But some later efforts are unintelligible. He has real insight, and even in situations where he doesn't have a subject or a predicate, he at least points to a matter that people haven't noticed before. He causes you to think some new thoughts even if they don't come directly from him.

I can't help being fussy about what the turmoil in communications really means. It involves a lot more than just what is troubling business. There are problems between husband and wife in communicating, and between parents and children. There's a lot of distrust about whether people are saying what they mean or meaning what they say. It isn't just a question of commercial advertisers saying something that isn't so. I think, as a matter of fact, that some of the consumer discontent with advertisers has been a sort of proxy for a more basic distrust of everybody and everything. It's all very disturbing.

A lot of parents today have the experience of discovering very late that their kids have been fooling around with narcotics, and not only that but these parents find that they are being condemned for their attitudes at being distressed over this. They're being told that the reason they didn't know about it was that it was simply assumed that their reaction would be just what it was, which is a "stupid, old-fashioned, ignorant, prejudiced attitude." This also applies to current sexual behavior. Someone goes away to college and everything seems to be o.k. The money is arriving on schedule and the grades and the questions about how school is going are answered and then suddenly the family discovers that the offspring has been living with a member of the opposite sex for the past year. And the parents have been supporting this without realizing it.

The result of all this perhaps is that, as Madison Avenue says, it is society which is at fault, not just the professional communicators. But I don't quite agree so broadly and categorically that society should be indicted. I think that the ordinary person discounts stuff from any commercial source. He expects a certain amount of overstatement and so he is on guard and he isn't too let down if he's taken in a little because that's part of the game.

I've always thought that the younger generation has absorbed all too well this notion to discount whatever is commercial. They are sophisticated, skeptical, tough customers to persuade of anything and those in the advertising field, the serious people giving their lives to it, must feel a little anxious.

Television is a medium that really troubles me. I think that TV has wasted its potential horribly. What it's done compared to what it might have done represents a terrible shortcoming, and if this ever hits people dramatically, the effect on the networks is going to be devastating. The broadcasters got rich too fast and began to congratulate themselves that they were really kings of everything and lost not only the ability to engage in criticism but lost any vision of what they hadn't

yet accomplished. They were too busy reaping the benefits of their apparent success. Success is very difficult
to argue with, even when based on the wrong premises.

There are all kinds of people who get elected to office
and take this as a marvelous endorsement of their own
virtues. And then at some point they are voted out of
office and they can't believe it. In the same way, the
realization by broadcasters of what they have sadly
failed to do will come from the outside. It won't come
through the dawning of insight from people inside
television that they have failed disastrously to recognize
some of the great things that they might have attempted
and accomplished.

In the media, the reporting is so standardized that you
could really publish it in the newspaper with the names
changed. It would be the same as years ago, an actress's
jewels are stolen or whatever, and often you wonder,
from the way it's reported and standardized, if someone
hasn't taken it out of the old files. We all know that a lot
of people consume that sort of thing in quantity and so
a lot of other people produce it and apparently enjoy
doing it. In a certain sense, the community is victimized
by stereotypes propagated by the media, and certainly
the reporting of crime is so standardized that it is laugh-
able. It's not just the commercial advertisers who tell us
what the world is like, who form our ideas. Everyone is
in the position of relaying certain things to others and
in so doing giving a false impression. This causes us to
think the way the others want us to think or to think of
them the way they want to be thought of. What's needed
is more personal exposure so that people know better
what is really going on so they can become more skepti-

cal. I don't mean this from the sense of cultivating distrust but to distinguish between first-hand experience and the picture that is conveyed in the media.

Among other things this would make the public realize how difficult it is to communicate a true picture, because the public is very impatient and certainly college students are full of prejudices and very intolerant. I'm astonished by the picture a lot of them have of the big corporations. I've probably spent too many years inside them and I know first-hand a lot about them. And while there is reason enough for young people to be skeptical, some of the charges they make and the picture they have of what goes on in the inside is miles from reality and they don't know it. They have sense enough to disbelieve some of the charges made by, say, the militants, but not the sense of what they can accept as an alternative.

SMITH: WHO'LL BE
THE JUDGE?

Selling the product based on its own merits is the heart of the issue. Somehow, when you wander about Madison Avenue or look at the comments and citations of those who are critical of it, you get a view of the role of advertising which is so overwhelming as to imply that it is true that it controls almost everything. But when you work in the industry and expose consumers to questions, you learn very quickly that that is grossly overstated.

Indeed, as you work on the materials that Madison

Avenue uses, you find that it is very difficult to get some-one to pay attention to you. It is damned near impossible to get people to read your message fully and it is extraordinarily difficult to communicate fully the ideas you wish to in the context of the sort of crowded, jammed, pufferied environment that advertising creates. And if you look at a typical advertisement, you find that an enormous portion of the audience to which it was addressed didn't even see it and that there are a variety of mechanisms with which people shut you out and this is far more common than Madison Avenue would like to acknowledge.

Critics like you say that what we really should do is to have products exhibited and acquired on the basis of their own merits. Well, when you start pushing at that argument, it gets very, very subtle. Whose perception of the merit and what is a merit? Bread just on the basis of its nutrients? Well, how about quality, texture, taste, sugar content, et cetera. And what about clothing, on the basis of merit, durability, style, fit? There are all sorts of intangible, terribly personal, subjective judgments involved. I am profoundly reluctant to have someone else decide for me what the merits of a proposition are and to guide me to make my judgments on a product— whether that somebody is in Washington or in a corporate headquarters.

If you take some of the arguments made by the FTC— and I don't mean the commissioners but the staff in working papers that I have seen—puffery is going to be eliminated to some degree. You'll have a simple blanket statement on what the product attributes are. Think about that for a moment. They will have to be presented with some sort of typeface and I submit that different typefaces do indeed communicate differently. Old English as against long, slender modern letters delivers a whole new message. One reason for this is our experience in society. We know what is associated with what. People bring with them to the graphics and the language of an ad, and to the statement of product attributes, a whole set of values which shape the meanings that they take from them. No one can make that judgment for them. No one can control it.

Let's talk about TV commercials. I've got illustrations over and over again of entire commercial campaigns for which the best that can be said is that they didn't do any real harm to the product. I have illustrations of corporate imagery campaigns where the consequence was to enhance the stature of the principal competitor. In one case, a company took a major corporate institutional campaign largely to inform the business community of its breadth, its diversity, its expertise. But, in measuring the consequences of the campaign, we discovered that the company ended up slightly lower in the esteem of the people than it wanted to influence.

Let me say this, too. Clearly, there are abuses, gross abuses. How do you draw the line? I think there is some garishly vulgar advertising. I think lies, frank lies, should be eliminated. And just as we protect children from the abuses of child labor, I think they should be protected from communications that are grossly misleading to them.

I don't like the sex in airline advertising or the use of phallic symbols for men's toiletries. I think by and large these efforts to induce a sexual ambience are silly. They will not do the job they are intended to do.

But rather than creating them, I think our communicators are reading the signals which are developing and then playing to them. That is to say, there is great sexual freedom—not just in the United States but all over—it's a worldwide permissiveness; there is a modification in clothing, an increasing disposition to develop a more "acceptant" attitude toward all sorts of perverse behavior. All this is certainly not to be laid at the feet of the communicators. What they are doing is simply making note of it. So I think our communications systems are indicted falsely as being central to those changes, since all they do is make them more evident—at least more evident than if we did not have a professional communications business which reads as its job the taking of the temperature of this society and then using what it learns from those readings to help sell products, services and corporate or personal identities.

I think that what is at issue basically is how much reliance do you have on the essential wit and good sense of the American public? How much need they be protected from the error of their own ways? My nervousness about that is that I don't know who the protectors are going to be and that always scares me. I've had many meetings with young FTC attorneys whom I find diligent, concerned and committed, and wholly unaware of the consequences of some of the actions that they propose.

For example, there is great discussion going on as to what redress should be asked from advertisers whose work is found unacceptable. One of the views, let us say illustrative only, is that for an analgesic you cannot say it is "faster," since all analgesics are comparably fast.

Let's make a blanket rule in the industry, those attorneys say, that "faster" cannot be used as a claim. But it may well be that one of the products in that field has claimed its "faster" characteristic throughout its history and is central to its success. By making a blanket enjoinder from using the "faster" claim, you inflict preferential damage on one brand rather than another. I'm not saying that you shouldn't do that, only that we should examine the consequences of such an action before we take it.

Very often what a consumer needs and what rewards he gets are not immediately apparent to us. Clearly, cigarettes serve some important purpose to the human beast and clearly he is aware of their potential danger. But cigarettes are selling as well, if not better, than ever. And what about the matter of nonleaded gasolines, the low-lead gasolines which were clearly to help the pollution problem, products made at a formidable cost? The consumer, despite his assertions regarding the importance of the pollution issue, isn't buying the gasoline. It reestablishes once again the consumer's disposition to do his own thing, even though we do not know why.

# II.

## Foisting
## the Fantasy
## as Reality

# 5.

## The
## Coming of
## the Come-On

### THE MOOD WORSENS

IN THE SEVENTIES—or just a bit more than a quarter-century since the modern come-on began—Americans were clearly getting fed up.

Before the Vietnam war was settled, there was an outpouring of self-flagellation about the decline of American society. Rarely was there such pessimism, so much breast-beating over the alienation between the people and their institutions, about the lack of believability of our power structure and on the loss of momentum in our national goals.

If you were to take seriously both the humble and the pontifical admonitions and all the statistics pumped out by the demographic samplings, you would have to conclude that the country and the society were teetering on the brink of oblivion.

The Watergate scandals in which Republican zealots broke in, bugged and stole documents from the Democratic headquarters in Washington fell like an avalanche on the heads of the American public in late 1972 and occupied much of the time and efforts of the media through 1973. Those revelations included others of like shock—forged letters sent on the stationery of at least one opposing candidate in the 1972 Presidential primary, rumors fed and nourished that two Democratic candidates had engaged in illicit sexual acts, use of the FBI and the CIA to ferret out secrets of the Democrats, illegal campaign contributions aimed at obtaining a favorable ruling from a Federal agency, *ad infinitum.*

Yet by the time the Senate committee opened formal hearings on the Watergate disclosures, the public was already sated by the overabundant coverage. Ratings on the televised coverage of the committee hearings showed that soap operas were getting a greater audience. There was just so much that the senses could take. By that time, it was already evident that the public simply wanted to hide in the banalities of soap operas and nighttime cops-and-robbers series. The fictional had become preferable to the horribly factual.

But the public wasn't to have its way. Columnists, historians, pollsters, philosophers and psychologists insisted on knowing why the fabric of society was being ripped apart.

Anxious to find out what had happened to the revolutionary trends in the country during the early sixties, Max Lerner, the historian and columnist, decided that a "trial balance" was being struck by one or both of two coexisting theories.

"One is that all the chaos of changes adds up to a disintegration of America," he said, "not immediately but before the end of the century—its energies run down, its values corrupted, its unity split, its will to survive stymied."

Lerner's other theory was that America was going through convulsive, dislocating changes which led to many discontents, that the civilization may well fall victim to these changes and discontents, though there is a good chance to survive them and emerge a stronger rather than a weaker civilization. But, said Lerner, "I can't prove this view nor do I discount the opposite one."

Wondering whether Americans were not talking too much and saying too little, Daniel J. Boorstin, a major historian, author and director of the National Museum of History and Technology of the Smithsonian Institution, observed, "In our world of calloused ears and over-taxed eyes, there are many symptoms of the desperate need of people to make somebody listen, to be sure somehow that somebody is hearing.

"More and more people are willing to pay fees they cannot afford to medically trained psychiatric listeners who listen, nod and take notes. More and more desperate people, especially young people with great energy who find that they cannot get people to listen when they do say something, decided instead and perhaps understandably to throw something. . . . With the rise of photography and the movies, of radio and television, and with the improvement and diffusion of the graphic arts, a larger and larger proportion of what is to be communicated has to be vivid. To catch and hold our attention, the images must be in motion. So it is not surprising that more and more of what is communicated to us is explosive and disruptive, interrupting the current of our experience."

At about the same time, an extraordinary eighteen-hour seminar was held in Paris by the French Finance Ministry in which philosophers, futurologists, statesmen and businessmen from a dozen countries met to examine what was wrong with industrial society. There were articulate pessimists such as Sicco Mansholt, former president of the European Common Market's executive commission in Brussels, who foresaw the catastrophe that would face mankind if national economic growth rates were not curbed. The Dutch socialist warned that "man is already in the shadow" and capitalist society cannot deal with the condition.

But there were optimists too. Bertrand de Jouvenel, a French philosopher, said that man had noble instincts but that his problems were essentially moral, rooted in the alienation man feels from large organizations that no longer give employees pride in their work.

Three basic schools of thought emerged before the conference ended: (1) something had to be done about growth; (2) nothing had to be done about growth; (3) something had to be done but not very much. Most participants, in eyeing the problems of world society, agreed that changes in the direction if not in the structure of society were needed to restore industrial man's sanity and stability.

But if the conditions of international society were troublesome to a distinguished international conference, a trio of independent samplings of Americans at about the same time indicated a clear worsening in their attitude about their own power structure, the business establishment and their faith in their own importance in contemporary society.

In a study of public attitudes toward 20 major occupations among more than 400 people by a team of University of Connecticut psychologists, professionals such as physicians, clergymen, dentists, judges, psychologists and college professors received the most votes for truthfulness, in that order. On a ranking of 20, businessmen placed 13th, U.S. Army generals 14th, TV repairmen 15th, newspaper columnists 16th, auto repairmen 17th, labor-union officials 18th, politicians 19th and used-car salesmen 20th.

"Big corporations face the worst attitude climate in a decade," reported Opinion Research Corporation, Princeton, New Jersey, after a national sampling that measured the views of 4,059 persons. The responses indicated a variety of misconceptions leading to suspicion and distrust among the respondents on corporate after-tax profits, price increases and the need for government to control profits. One-third of the respondents were convinced that workers' standards of living should be raised by getting a larger share of the corporate revenue rather than by increasing their own productivity.

And in a poll by Louis Harris, results showed that feelings of alienation among Americans had risen from 40 percent to 47 percent between 1971 and 1972. Asked for their reaction on "The rich get richer and the poor get poorer," 68 percent agreed against 62 percent concurring in 1971 and 54 percent in 1968. On the point "The people running the country don't really care what happens to people like yourself," 50 percent agreed, compared with 41 percent in 1971 and 36 percent in 1968. And asked how they felt about "People who have the power are out to take advantage of you," 38 percent agreed compared with 33 percent in 1971.

Clearly, Americans were disillusioned on many fronts.

### THE COMMUNICATORS REACT

The quality of life in a society is determined by the quality of its culture. Ours is rotten. The advertising industry has helped create it and is continuing to make it worse.

If advertising responded positively to the consumerism movement, the resultant effectiveness of ads could save all industry two billion dollars a year. As people become more confident that ads are truthful, there will be a reduction in the numbers and impact, if not the elimination, of many of the charlatans in our business.

These statements, which occasioned more than a few angry rebuttals from advertising men, were not made by Ralph Nader, the chief of the consumerism advocates, or by doctrinaire critics of the advertising business. They were made by prominent advertising practitioners. The first comment came from Milton Marcus, vice president of Claire Advertising Agency. The second was made by Arthur W. Schultz, chairman of Foote, Cone, & Belding Communications, Inc.

But some other communicators I spoke to were candid in their own way, too.

"Don't Americans ask for oversell and overplay?" said Jim Cope, chairman of Selvage, Lee and Howard, one of the top public-relations agencies in New York. "Conglomerates have been an oversell and an overbuy for years. When they fell on their face, not everyone yelled. Many people shrugged. After all, they implied, the concept was a gamble. . . . Blacks, too, are enormously proud that Muhammad Ali and Joe Frazier are the top professional fighters in the world today. They hope that the two men will be a credit to their race as their careers progress, but even if they, too, should fall on their faces, if there should be any stigma to what they did, so what?"

Other comments at random:

> One of the biggest hoaxes in public relations are the phony blue-sky promises. The prospective client is lured by the assurance that signing with the agency will quickly result in getting him on the cover of *Time* or *Business Week*—or at least an article in the *New York Times* magazine. This reflects a serious weakness of the PR business— the top agency people are salesmen, not placement or production people who know most intimately what it takes to turn out a successful PR effort (*Len Kessler,* Doremus Company, New York).

> There's more BS in public relations per square inch than in any other business I know of—with the exception of advertising, law, accounting and so on. I'm not bothered as much by the inflated image that the business tries to get away with as by the distorted manner in which lots of PR

men use the media and get away with it (*Jack Bernstein,* president of Jack Bernstein Associates, New York).

You can say it as much as you like—you can't create an image if there isn't anything solid behind it. You just can't take something that isn't there and build a house around it—or a personality that just doesn't have one. If the client is a *schmuck*, do you think you can build him into a genius? No, a *schmuck* is a *schmuck*—and the same goes for a company. If it has poor labor relations, poor-quality products, if it's behind the times, if it's unscrupulous, you just can't create a reverse image. But if you have something to work on, something to market, maybe you can do something with it (*Allan T. Zachary*, president, Zachary and Front, Inc., New York).

Advertising's intentions are good—but the execution is bad (*Jack O'Dwyer,* publisher of an advertising news letter and advertising columnist for the *Chicago Tribune*).

Imagery is what the advertising business is selling, rather than technically good or quality advertisements. ... Our industry has given lip-service to the need for self-regulations ... the government has made a good case of the need for regulation and finally managements of agencies and clients are being compelled to respond to the issues of consumerism (*John Rockwell*, president of John Rockwell Associates, New York).

Packages produce sensations. The effect of the package is in the realm of perception, impact and psychological connotations. Packages are not works of art; they are selling tools produced by individuals who have been trained to use plastics and graphics to communicate and to motivate. Only by implementing scientific methodology can we determine the effect of a package—its impact, the sensation it produces, the attitudes of consumers toward the package or the product in the package. To depend on the judgment of a designer, a marketing expert, a brand manager or company executive is to court marketing disaster (*Louis Cheskin*, Louis Cheskin Associates, Chicago).

Advertising is in the business of training consumers. Denouncing advertising is like denouncing a pimple instead of denouncing the way we live. Let's face it for once—advertising is to our culture as our culture is to our moral code (*Martin Solow*, former president of Solow/Wexton, Inc., New York).

Yes, no—maybe? Am I hurting my premise? Perhaps so in giving you a spectrum of comment in these random quotes. But I promised a full debate in this volume.

### THE PLOYS BEGAN BEFORE YESTERDAY

At the outset of this chapter I observed that the modern come-on began roughly twenty-five years ago or, broadly speaking, when World War II ended in 1945. As Professor Nelson Foote of Hunter College pointed out earlier, P. T. Barnum was a pioneer in the put-on, humbug effort during the nineteenth century, capable of turning some questionable artists into worldwide personalities. The era of hustling show business followed in that vein, continuing through the following decades. Then there were the financial con artists who fooled millions in the twenties and thirties, such as Philip Musica, who successfully led a double-life, first as a wig importer and then as the man who defrauded the pharmaceutical firm of McKesson-Robbins; Ivar Kreuger, the match king, who duped many a stockholder on both sides of the Atlantic; and Samuel Insull, the utilities king, who did likewise.

The thirties were a dizzy and dangerous time. Between the depth of the depression, 1932, and the most critical year, 1939, when the country seemed to teeter hazardously between chaos and relief as war threatened in two hemispheres, there was scarcely more than half a decade. But in the years that followed through the end of the big war, the pendulum swung from need-and-want for the masses to have-but-crave for goods made scarce by the war effort. The biggest seller's market of all time, from 1940 through 1946, reversed the come-on technique, with one exception.

The persuasion that emanated from the White House in the dulcet, aristocratic tones of a President in a wheelchair provided a one-to-one communication that has probably never been equaled in this country. Without the urgency that came two years later when Pearl Harbor was bombed, he spoke simply: "Never before . . . has our American civilization been in such danger as now." What had to be done? More arms, more planes, tanks, guns, freighters and soon probably rationing of consumer and luxury goods. Concluded Franklin Delano Roosevelt, "We must be the great arsenal of democracy." It was an effective summoning to arms.

The late thirties and a good part of the forties were

marked by big blobs of corn flung over the radio, mixed with solid, apple-pie humor. "Kay Kyser's Kollege of Musical Knowledge" and "Your Hit Parade" were tops on radio and kept millions glued to their parlors on the nights the shows were broadcast. A skinny baritone with a prominent Adam's apple wowed the teen-agers and Frank Sinatra's long, long career was under way. And so was that of a pointy-nosed comic who was eventually to become one of America's richest men, Bob Hope, star of radio, the movies, television and, eventually, "The Late Show."

When the war finally ended, so did the way Americans lived. By 1950, the pipelines were largely filled for big-ticket goods. But the big appliance boom was satisfied, as was the demand for cars, even homes for the time being. The discount house came in, the influx of people to the suburbs was already well under way and in only a few short years the Supreme Court would declare its momentous judgment on equality for minorities in housing and education. A belated maturity appeared to be setting in in those scant few years after World War II and the involvement in Korea—a yearning for peace of mind; for the right to live quietly and fruitfully without war, casualties and scarcities; and for a while it all seemed possible and at hand. Americans, it developed, were doing so well that they launched history's biggest movement to help underdeveloped, war-torn countries, even former enemies, an effort that lasted two decades and more. We were the world's affluent benefactors.

But if we were changing outwardly, the inward changes were even more marked. The average American was eating better, drinking better beer and a wider variety of scotch and bourbon; and he was banking more and found himself fully capable of paying his rent and mortgage. The recessions of 1958, 1962, 1968 through 1970 were years away. He was, for the time, satisfied in his material wants but he was troubled by the shadow that was soon to become an immense hovering cloud— his safety and his family's safety. The traumatic experience of our use of the atomic bomb during the war lingered, perhaps made as much a part of his consciousness by the debate that waxed around the country as by his own subconscious fears and memories of the mushroom figure.

How to distract a man with a full belly and a troubled conscience? Or, perhaps more important, how do you entice the man who has everything but vaguely wants something—but what? This was what occupied the attention of the admen, the sales-promotion experts, the public-relations practitioners and especially their employers. It also, not very parenthetically, occupied the thinkers, politicians and image makers in Washington and the state capitals.

The answer, of course—developed through considerably sweaty, costly trial-and-error—was the gimmicky put-on; the quasi-humorous, quasi-facetious, quasi-worrisome exaggeration. It was a compound of "Look, you need something to pep you up, so why not this?" and "Of course, we're kidding you, mainly because we're so sure of the superiority of what we're selling we can even kid ourselves about it" and "Pull yourself together, buster, it's later than you think, so enjoy a little."

It worked like the proverbial charm, mostly anyway,

with some exceptions like the Edsel, a handful of packaged products, toothpaste, shaving cream and so on, and, of course, two more recent presidents, Johnson and Nixon.

SOME OF THE MORE-OR-LESS
NOTABLE COME-ONS AND
PUT-ONS OF THE 1950S
AND 1960S

A perennial nominee, Henry Krajewski, the "People's Candidate," ran for President at least twice and for senator from New Jersey when he polled 35,000 votes to keep the incumbent to a puny plurality of only 3,000 votes. Also known as the "Pig Farmer from Secaucus," Krajewski left school in the fifth grade and as the oldest of nine children went to work to help support his family. Climbing up from the pigsties of Secaucus, he made a small fortune by picking up the swill and garbage from local factories and restaurants. Politics interested him because he felt that as a fellow who had surmounted poverty, he could lead a "Poor Man's Party."

Wearing a ten-gallon Western hat and campaigning in a Cadillac painted red, white and blue, and with his garbage trucks bearing his banners, he began to believe that he had a chance to win. While running against Eisenhower, John F. Kennedy and Senator Clifford Case, he held forth in his tavern in the meadowlands of New Jersey, surrounded by his cohorts. But while everyone recognized his candidacy for what it was—a big joke—the notoriety which promoted his business in the tavern made him rich. Once the Associated Press took him seriously, requesting a telephone interview on "Why should we be in Korea?" But his closest friends—and a public-relations man who helped him—compelled him to refuse. Henry, it appeared, had never learned to improve his speech. Through all his campaigning, he still spoke with "dems and dese." So the request was never granted.

And, during those years, there were all those important committees, supposedly representing strongly based coalitions of citizens. Like the Independent Committee for the Secession of Staten Island from New York City—run solely by a sixteen-year-old boy.

And the institutes and "culture societies," which were in reality created full-born from the fertile, conniving mind of some public-relations man entirely in the interests of one of his clients. How many "Fashion Institutes" has the public been belabored with, or adaptations thereof, which purported to name the ten best-dressed men, women, entertainers and—monkeys?

And the nutritional institutes, "no load" financial groups, vaguely defined citizens' committees and specialized research foundations whose activities and aims were so esoteric that even the most naive person was impressed, for a while, at least.

In those two decades, as one veteran New York PR consultant put it, wisely requesting anonymity, "It was all so easy. A good front, an impressive letterhead, an important-sounding name—and all of a sudden you were either a pressure group or a public institution."

And all the business gimmicks—a pagoda phone

booth in New York's Chinatown; overcoming the problems of Christmas giftwrapping by showing how easily a blind person could do it; Willie Sutton, the famed bank robber, proclaiming that a particular safe made safes safe; making the doughnut-dunking effort socially acceptable by showing Emily Post dunking one but breaking the doughnut in two first, of course; and, not to be ignored, the stunt that put the Renault car across in the United States.

For decades, Renault, a French firm, had one of the most respected names in the European automobile industry. During World War I, the company had built French Army tanks and during World War II military vehicles. After that war, eyeing the big demand in the United States for new cars, Renault decided to try to crack the American market. But others had the idea first—Volkswagen, the British MG and Austin—and Renault was unable to mount a bold entry.

A small but hustling public relations firm was hired to help. It found that Renault had image problems. Americans, at least the Americans who might be potential Renault buyers, thought that the French were a nation of hand kissers, wine drinkers and dress designers. The fact that the French had a heavy industry or, for that matter, a major automobile manufacturer, never occurred to the average American consumer.

The PR firm told the client that a dramatic touch was needed. Renault then gave its go-ahead to a project that was aimed at reversing Renault's hazy image and so-so sales within five days.

An American couple was hired to drive a Renault car nonstop across the country. The couple, both skilled drivers, spelled each other at the wheel on the New York-to-California round trip, driving twenty-four hours a day, and stopping only for gas or the call of nature. The drivers lost a half hour in Milwaukee for gas and minor adjustments, but mainly because they were swamped in the station by autograph hunters. The car also sustained a flat tire in the Mojave Desert. But the couple finished the six thousand mile trip in five days, four hours and twenty minutes.

Prompted by constant releases and communiqués, the nation's newspapers outdid themselves. Hundreds carried the story on their front pages virtually from coast to coast. The major wire services issued two daily bulletins on the couple's progress.

At the end of the fifth day, Renault dealers had almost no cars left. Many were sold out for several months ahead. The momentum built up from the stunt until, within a few years, Renault was selling sixty thousand cars annually to the American market. The gimmick established that France did have a heavy industry, had the know-how and manufacturing capability to produce an economy vehicle which could sustain prolonged use under hazardous driving conditions.

But the success was not to last. Renault ran into difficulties because of inadequate American service facilities and sales fell off. The PR firm was dropped in favor of a larger, more prestigious publicist. The small PR outfit wasn't the only one to suffer a reverse, however. A year after the trip, the couple that drove cross-country was divorced. Inescapable conclusion: if you and your wife ever want to traverse the country nonstop and return in five days, four hours and twenty minutes, don't drive a Renault. Take an airplane.

Then there were the games, lotteries, "contests" of both decades, come-ons that were somehow in tune with the time. Combined with entertainment, use of celebrities and considerable razzle-dazzle, television programs such as "Stop the Music" and "Sing It Again" entrapped willing millions, while a wave of lotteries and the giveaway of valuables by major marketing companies ensnared almost as many more. With the latter, at least, the deceptive nature lay in the fact that moneys and gifts offered depended upon subscriptions, purchases or the answering of solicitations. If these efforts were not as productive as the sponsors hoped, only a percentage of the total advertised prizes were distributed. After years, the Federal Trade Commission stepped in and compelled the sponsoring companies to distribute all the gifts and sums they advertised and to publish a list of winners supplied on request to any interested parties. But the stringencies dismayed many, and some sponsors, particularly Procter & Gamble, canceled their giveaways.

The television giveaways, however, avoided the restriction and only stopped functioning when the public lost interest. Broadcasting lotteries are prohibited by federal laws. The Federal Communications Commission tried to kill the airing of such giveaway shows as "Stop the Music" and "Sing It Again" on the basis that the at-home participants were engaged in a lottery. The U.S. Supreme Court agreed with the commission but found against any injunction voiding the radio and TV shows. The High Court ruled that listening to the radio or watching television in the home did not represent an element essential to a lottery. Viewing the participant's involvement, which included either registering free in a retail store or waiting for a drawing at a specified location, the Supreme Court said that no one had paid, bought or done anything other than listen to a communications medium.

Seen from the standpoint of the average fan of the media, who tuned in to the giveaway shows by the millions, the Court's decision was undoubtedly popular and lenient. But the public made up its own mind when it wearied over the airborne giveaways.

A somewhat different reason prompted the viewer to lose interest in the most famous television quiz show of the time. For several years, the TV show "The $64,000 Question" drew the highest ratings for televiewer popularity. But fraud and manipulation involved in the awards cast a cloud over the weekly show, occasioning considerable criticism in the industry and in the press. Credibility shriveled and the show languished.

The two decades of image making, the come-on, put-on variety, was also marked by a widespread use of testimonials from famous entertainers, athletes and socialites on every imaginable product and service. The endorsements ranged from assertions that their life had been beautified to confessions that only by application of the wonderful product had they been saved from a life of dullness and boredom. Later, in the 1970s, the networks elected not to identify the endorser, believing and hoping that a simple view of a famous face or hearing a well-known voice would have more believability in pushing the product. But what they didn't count on were the kinks in programming which have the famous movie-star grappling for his life at the break for the commercial and then immediately seen in his own den endorsing coffee, aspirin or cold tablets. Time gap? The public will understand and forgive, so they hope.

But should the public forgive and forget the fraud that was foisted on it by the televised quiz shows? "The downfall of rigged quiz shows and the revelations of widespread payola practices in broadcasting brought to the surface a public distrust of the broadcast media which was wider than many informed observers had suspected," declared Earl W. Kintner, former chairman of the FTC, in his 1971 book, *A Primer on the Law of Deceptive Practices.*

"Television, after all, is a peculiarly intimate medium. It brings simultaneous sight and sound into the living room before an audience of all ages. This intimacy makes television all the more vulnerable to public criticism for possible abuses of its responsibility. The entire broadcasting industry thus owes to the public and to itself a most rigorous and searching variety of self-regulation. The broadcasting industry cannot afford to shrug off public cynicism with the attitude that 'it will all blow over.' It has not blown over and will not blow over."

On television advertising, Kintner has a few succinct words: "Much of TV advertising is thoroughly disgusting and shows up most advertising men as cultural nitwits."

In their scope and endless variety, the lures of the marketplace and the awesome lies pushed on the public of the 1950s and '60s could easily fill a book of their own. But the foregoing will offer some flavor of what went on. Oddly enough a number of the advertising men I interviewed in the course of researching this book looked back nostalgically on the 1960s and said they regard the advertising of that decade as "creative . . . colorful . . . stimulating . . . effective." By contrast, the scrutiny by the FTC and the increasing cries from the consumerists have turned advertising dull and conservative in the 1970s, the same advertising practitioners complain. Who wants to be different anymore and thus stand out from the herd of sheep when the hounds are out?

I suggest that is not what has happened at all, not merely in advertising but in various types of communications of a major nature. Deceptions continue unabated, government restrictions notwithstanding. In fact, if the perpetrations of the 1950s and '60s justifiably concerned the public and the government, there is just as much reason for concern in the 1970s.

Maybe more so.

# 6.

## The Sensual Desensitizing of the 1970s

THE HAPPIEST man in the world.

—Who is he? He's the little old retiree who lives with his smiling, contented wife in a tiny, paid-up house, his children having satisfactorily married, and his lawn a slim rectangle that he has neutralized into a rock garden. Deliberately he disposed of his television set, has only a huge, forty-year-old Philco radio with a rounded top and tiny dial on which he listens only to the baseball games. He turns the volume down when the commercials come on, smiling primly like a man who has made his peace with the world. For years, his only other form of reading matter has been the *Reader's Digest*. He has little to do with his neighbors (they are all of the same ethnic background he is) except to nod and briefly discuss the weather. Social Security, Medicaid, lean but adequate savings, occasional walks around the neighborhood, poking at the rock garden, a contented companionship with his bustling wife, going to sleep at ten —these are the cornerstones of the happy man's life.

He does not exist, of course. And if he did, he would be a vegetable. But we do exist, and what is our happiness and vegetable quotient?

In this tense, unhappy, frantic America of ours, it is possible to be happy if one is a vegetable but that is clearly impossible. On all sides, each of us is bombarded by behavior and communications double-binds (noncommunications consisting, if you recall, of two messages of opposing nature) and by our own instinctive reactions to internal deficits that we try, often vainly, to satisfy in the external world. But perhaps the real bombardment comes from our total environment in which every commercial, entertainment, cultural, governmental and institutional element of our society is busily engaged in selling itself. There is nothing wrong with this in itself but it is in the selling "pitch," the sales approach, that we are being desensitized, being made nonreactive to "sensitizing" agents. Those agents are hard-sell appeals to our sexual, mercenary, hedonistic, noncultural, violence-prone instincts on one side, and on the other to our familial, communal, keep-the-cave-inviolate instincts. But the first, the base, sensual pitches are much more common than the second, the home-family protective pitches. At the same time, the stress on the sensuous rather than on the truthful, factual and logical in a world when only the truthful, factual and logical will keep us rational has resulted in a diminishing of our values, another phase of the desensitizing process. In a word, we are losing our values because our values are being manipulated by others with specific, ulterior motives.

The result of this pervasive desensitizing is our growing callousness to all we perceive. The overwhelming response to the grand deception confronting all of us is an almost complete loss of credibility in not only all our communications elements but also in the various institutions in American society.

And furthermore, the desensitizing of our emotions and taste and steady erosion of our values—all coming at us in the form of communications implied, direct and behavioristic—is compelling us to play the personal game of deception mentioned earlier. The assault on our basic instincts over many generations of human behavior must also have an adverse effect on our personal relationships with others on all levels of intimacy.

Not only is the sensual bombardment affecting the young—even the very young—but the mature as well. The effects on the young and on adults are different and subtle. But they are evident nonetheless, altering such important interhuman relationships as consideration toward other age groups, the other sex, other races and income differences, and in general, toward ethics and morals. Trying to shake off the attack on our senses and instincts by the communicators, government and business, it is sometimes difficult to face one's family, one's coworkers, one's neighbors, one's juniors without masking the sheepish grin behind which lies some real pain. Psychic and emotional pain can be even harder to bear than physical pain, although you may not die of it.

Generalities aside, let's examine how it all works, what the assault is and how it affects people. Touches of this appeared in the second chapter, but now I will direct a more intense spotlight on a microcosm of the problem from the standpoint of two adult members of a typical middle-income American family, fictional, of course.

The Harmons live in a suburb of a major city, subsisting on a family income of about $22,500 which leaves them in relatively secure but not affluent circumstances. The family consists of Jack and Katie Harmon, both in their early forties; Richard, twenty-two, an executive trainee in a large corporation; and Jill, seventeen, a high-school senior. Jack graduated from a local college with a business administration degree; his wife left the same school after only two years to marry him. The family has traveled throughout much of the country and the parents have been to Europe once and to the Virgin Islands once.

### The Man in the
### Double-Knit Suit

Glancing back for a moment at the neat, small colonial house that he has just left, Jack Harmon felt a sudden sense of pleasure and self-accomplishment. He had been sold on the house from the first moment, although Katie had felt it was one-third more in price than they could afford. But he was managing it without incurring too much more debt. At that moment, his wife and daughter emerged and they waved to him. He waved back, stilling the quickening of his pulse at the last sight of them.

The news on the radio as he had dressed was as disquieting as ever. The reports of crime, the war, inflation, the confusion that emanated from Washington had drifted around him like dark clouds and he had tried to isolate himself from them. "Have you prepared for your family's needs if you should die unexpectedly?" the announcer had asked in a sly but confident voice. Disinclined to answer, he had switched to another station, only to hear three consecutive sales pitches involving personal loans, cars and waterproofing the home. He had half-heard these but they had annoyed him a bit because it reminded him again how he had gradually come to feel about the radio nowadays—endless commercials interspersed with occasional music and comment.

As the tall, spare man in the light-blue double-knit suit with checks descended somewhat later to the subway, the irritation with radio commercials was hardly uppermost on his mind. A montage of concerns whipped through his consciousness, not constantly but whenever he put aside the newspaper to glance absently at his fellow riders. The impersonality that he felt toward strangers allowed the concerns to emerge. Not necessarily in order of importance, they involved Katie's recent breast pains, the restlessness of Richard, his son, Jill's presence in a troubled school, his own career uncertainty, his widowed mother's current illness. The newspaper was no consolation, he thought, but then it wasn't supposed to be, he told himself. But it was certainly incongruous in some odd way how the runovers of crime, rape, fraud, political shenanigans from the front and forward pages appeared alongside or near large ads featuring the latest fashions on giant figures that seemed to be 90 percent composed of legs. What the hell, he thought, who cares?

He was obviously not in the best of moods. He put his paper down again, trying to figure out what was really bothering him. Harmon's eyes moved to the car cards, and it did not amuse him that two of the three radio commercials that had irked him that morning had their counterparts on the car billboards. His glance fell on two of the other riders. One was a skinny youth of about twenty-three in faded jeans, with his long hair in a bun tied with a string, wearing a swastika hanging from another string around his neck. The kid was staring at Harmon with what seemed to him unquestionable derision. As he returned the youth's stare eyeball for eyeball, the boy's unswerving glare and certain hatred seemed to say, "You fucking white-collar guy, we'll get to you." The crossfire of stares lasted about forty-five seconds whereupon the youth withdrew by putting his right thumb knuckle in his mouth and biting down hard. The meaning was obvious to both of them.

Irked now more than he had been all morning, Harmon jarred his attention to the other rider who had caught his eye. This was a thin, stooped old man holding a cup in one hand and a heavy cane in the other which he banged heavily into the floor as he slowly, worriedly, moved forward. As he inched along, the beggar emitted a series of muted whelps, in the manner of "eeee, aieee," repeating them constantly, with a wagging of his head as though he were in pain or sorrow or both. He was a pitiful sight on the subway every day and at least every other morning Harmon dropped some coins into the beggar's cup. Only this time, as he groped for the coins, something strange happened. Harmon, who for some unknown reason had noticed before that the beggar's clothes were of good quality, pressed and neat, happened this time to glance at the man's shoes. They were polished to a high shine and easily the best-turned-out men's shoes in the car. Were they the shoes of a beggar —or those of a fraud? Something about the little old man with the apparently sightless eyes didn't ring true to Harmon, and he withheld his coins. And as the man moved by, drawing a steady flow of donations, the man in the double-knit suit didn't like himself any better for his suspicions. "Why do I have to feel that everyone is trying to sell me something or cheating me?" he asked himself.

In the office, he felt a little better. As a minor department head in a medium-size manufacturing company, he had his own little peaceful world of operations, planning and research and it had its own clear perimeters and rules. Harmon had a staff of six, with whom he had worked for ten years, and it was all harmonious. He worked for the corporate research and planning vice-president, Harvey Wallace, a decent, sensitive guy with whom he had always gotten along. But after he sat down at his desk, Harmon's secretary came in to tell that Wallace had come in earlier to say that he wanted to see him when he arrived.

It was not unusual, since Wallace got in a half hour

before he did and left a half hour earlier, but nonetheless Harmon's heart lurched momentarily. Was there some word on the transfer he wanted, the move to a higher-division job in the same city with more pay—or what? Was this the uncertainty that had been troubling him all morning? No, it wasn't.

Wallace was concentrating on some papers when Harmon was ushered into his office. He didn't look up for a moment. Obviously the papers were important. As he studied the stout, bald man who was so occupied, Harmon recalled that Wallace often made him wait in this manner. Finally the boss looked up, grinned and said, "Good morning, Jack. Boy, trying to make sense out of a mass of figures can be tough. You can take them two ways. How the hell are you?"

But his eyes weren't quite as friendly as his words. The lids were somewhat narrowed and no smile lit up Wallace's gray-blue pupils. "Jack," he said, slowly, "we've had some flak from the president on the report you submitted. He seems to feel that there's a lot of water in your estimates." Wallace got up and busied himself at the water cooler in the corner of his office. His back to Harmon, he added, "He seems to feel, too, Jack, that your department didn't exercise its usual care in drawing up the estimates." He returned with a paper cup full of water. "I told him, Jack, that I would discuss it with you and that I was sure you'd be happy to do it over and come back with lower estimates."

Harmon nodded, his heart pounding. "Sure," he replied, without enthusiasm. And then, because he knew for certain that his estimates had been realistic and that his department had exercised its usual care, he asked, defying the shaft that he surely invited, "Fine, Harvey. Any word on my request for the transfer?"

Wallace sat down hard in his chair, obviously irritated. He assembled the papers before him before answering and said, "To tell you the truth, Jack, I never submitted it. You see, when you ask the company to consider you for a move, especially a promotion, you've got to time it right. If the man had showed enthusiasm for your budget, I then would have submitted your request with a recommendation for approval. As it is, I can't do that. Timing, Jack, timing is everything."

The hard, gray-blue eyes took Harmon in, daring and perhaps inviting an argument. And he almost got it, too. Deep in him, Harmon knew that Wallace would never approve his transfer, because if he did he would lose the best department head he had and possibly the one guy who helped him keep his own job. But now, irritated because the one guy who could help him keep his own job had let him down with the president, Wallace wasn't pulling any punches. His own insecurity was showing through.

"All right, we'll come back with a better effort," Harmon said curtly and left.

Walking back to his own office, he knew that he would give his staff a hard time that day. It wasn't that he wanted to, but he knew himself enough to realize that inevitably his own mood communicated in tangible ways to the people who worked for him. He would try to absorb the brunt of the setback but he would, he knew instinctively, be unable to. And so it was.

Uncomfortable with himself most of the afternoon, he found some peace in the routine of the day, knowing he was seeking it. If there was a final irritation to his working day, it was when his secretary said that a Mr. Adams was phoning. Who was Mr. Adams? "Sounds like he knows you," she replied. He got on the phone and to his dismay found that he was talking to a life-insurance salesman. Because he had been unkind to his staff, he tried to be kind, although firm with Adams. That was a mistake. It took him five minutes, twenty seconds to get the leech off the phone. Not that the salesman wasn't smart and even subtle. "You know, Mr. Harmon, it's the provident guy who buys additional life insurance now in expectation of higher income later and in that way minimizes his premium," Adams said. "I hear tell you're a guy on the way up."

On the way down was more like it, Harmon thought. So, it was one of those days.

But there were no more incidents in the afternoon's last hour, no more incidents with Wallace, the staff, nor on the subway. On the way home he felt reasonably secure. He was still young enough to make a change if necessary, but he didn't think he would need to. Two years ago, after some really fine work on his part, the president of the company had written him in glowing terms of his future. "Nobody, dammit, can write that off," Harmon told himself, walking home, lanky and yet dapper in his light-blue knit suit that sort of swung with him.

Dinner was fine, as always. Katie stared at him occasionally with a sort of soft, liking expression, and Jill was quite pleasantly eager and pleasantly fresh to him. Richard, who had his own apartment in the city, phoned and was strangely noncommittal.

There was an hour of television, fifteen minutes of jerking a golf club at a ball in the back yard, before he settled down in the den for some homework on the troublesome estimates. The work defied him and he gave it up temporarily. He picked up the newspaper to scan the TV schedule, grimacing. One channel had a panel going in a few minutes on homosexuality; another had a commentator who was just then interviewing a famous lesbian; and two talk shows were also being aired. On the portable TV in the den, he gave each about five minutes. Doing so, he caught four sales pitches on feminine hygiene deodorants, beer and two brands of cigars. As always, he listened in disbelief:

> Sooner or later, you're gonna try a White Owl and when you do, we're gonna get ya! You know we're gonna get ya! You don't stand a chance! Would I lie?

> Should a gentleman offer a Tiparillo to a lady? And what if he does? . . . Tip-a-rillo tonight. . . .

Jack Harmon didn't smoke.

That night, after looking in on his daughter, sleeping calmly in her room, he slid into bed beside Katie. She was half asleep even though he was only five minutes into the bed after she was. "How do you feel?" he asked. "Wonderful," she breathed. He relaxed.

But he lay for an hour staring into the darkness. It had been a disturbing day, filled with irritants, abuses. And then he knew what it was that had been troubling him. He was losing his ability to cope—the ability to withstand the pressures and claims on him. At forty-two years of age? Then he laughed, laughed out loud in the quietness of the dark room. That was non-sense.

Tomorrow would be a better day, he thought, sure of it. It had to be.

## Mother Bravo

As her husband had left that morning, Katie Harmon, emerging with her daughter and waving at him, stared thoughtfully at his retreating figure. Jack was worried about so many things these days, her in particular, she thought, not to mention the children and his career. With a woman's instinct, she suspected that he would not get the new job he craved. She knew it because she had a way of listening between the words that Jack brought back to her. Why couldn't *they* talk straight to him instead of stringing him along?

"Let's go, Mother," said Jill at her side, "or we'll be late hitting the picket line."

Katie nodded, bracing herself for what she knew would be another unpleasant episode. A petite brunette with long hair in a ponytail, she strode to the five-year-old Plymouth that Jack had already driven out of the garage for her and got behind the wheel. Jill, a smaller copy of her mother, flounced in beside her. "All right, Katie," she said, "let's run the gauntlet."

Two miles away, Katie parked the car a block from the beige brick high-school building. As they approached the block-long structure, they could see a circular line of about twenty-five adults moving in front of the main entrance. A police car with two officers in it stood at the curb. A steady stream of youngsters went through the picket line, some of the line's members occasionally addressing them. It was not an unfamiliar scene in many major cities and their suburbs. With school decentralization having turned the schools' administration and selection of principals to the community, intracommunity differences had shown up, mostly along ethnic lines. At Jill's school, where a Negro assistant principal had been recently appointed, Spanish-Americans in the community now wanted equal representation with the appointment of a Spanish-American assistant principal, too.

As Jill went through the line, waving at Katie, one of the women in the line told Katie, "Why don't you support us? You got your white principal—don't we deserve a break, too?"

"What would you like me to do? Keep my child home?" Katie asked, calmly.

The picketer shrugged but a man on the line spoke up. "Yes, lady, that's what you should do, or maybe you don't care? Do you only care for yourself?"

As she drove away, Katie wondered how she would feel if she were in their shoes. As a "happy" WASP, she had always gotten along and it was difficult to put yourself in someone else's life, especially in an emotion-fraught situation. But she knew she would do nothing, having always objected in principle to school decentralization.

On the way home she detoured to a supermarket, a bit disturbed by the incident, and tried to concentrate on her shopping. But this was not easy. All the "cents off" and "twofer" banners, hung in series over counters themselves emblazoned with product blurbs, were distracting. She knew what she wanted, or thought she did, but she wound up buying more than she wanted to and later decided that she had been swayed into buying "bargains" that really weren't. Why don't *they* concentrate on nutrient value instead of on price? she wondered.

The rest of the morning consisted of cleaning up, briefly visiting a new neighbor, phoning Jack's ill mother, listening to the news on the radio (especially for any changes in the draft calls) and answering the front door twice. Once, it was the Avon lady, whom Katie quickly dispatched (she liked to buy her own cosmetics in her own good time), and the second time it was a vacuum-cleaner salesman, whom she also quickly got rid of. She already had two cleaners.

It was during her simple luncheon of a tuna-fish sandwich and coffee that she suddenly remembered for the first time that day—it was 1:25 P.M.—her breast pains. Yes, they were there, but were they anything? She had first become conscious of them when she saw a public-service commercial on TV warning of breast cancer. From then on, the pains had occurred intermittently, but she was sorry that she had ever mentioned them to Jack. He had enough on his mind. But someday soon, she would have to go to the doctor. At least, she told herself grimly, that was something constructive that TV had done.

At 1:45 the telephone rang. It was her son, Richard, his voice hot and irate.

"What's the matter, Dick?" she asked with concern.

He didn't answer right away. Then he blurted, "They

want me to spend a month out at the Indianapolis distribution center! They never mentioned it before. This morning, they called me in and said it was essential in our training, those two-faced hypocrites—"

As an executive trainee, Richard's indoctrination would last six months. Ordinarily, she would have thought that any young man would like a month away from home with pay, but in Richard's case she could understand his objection. Richard had a girl friend, Richard had a secondhand car, Richard had friends.

She finally calmed him down and he rang off. But the matter irked her. Business was pushing both her men. Richard was right: *they* had never given him advance notice until now that he would have to spend a month in Indianapolis. And in Jack's case, it was obvious to the Harmons that he was being strung along. Again, Katie asked herself, why couldn't *they* talk straight?

Suddenly, she felt slightly worn. It was 2:00 P.M. As if to immerse herself in blandness and refresh herself from lack of emotional exertion, she tuned in on NBC's "Days of Our Lives" on the TV in Jack's den. But it was *too* bland, *too* weepy, *too* melodramatic, *too* one-dimensional. She flipped the dial; same nonsense. A boob tube for boobs. She caught a commercial for feminine-hygiene deodorant and watched. It appealed to women to "be confident." Katie grinned. No one had ever complained.

At 3:00 P.M., she picked up Jill at the school. Mostly, Jill walked home but today Katie wanted to see her. Noticing that her daughter was downcast, Katie asked, "You, too? What's the matter?"

Jill grinned suddenly, sending a shaft of pain through

her mother. Why does she have to be so much like me? Katie wondered. That makes my concern for her even more to bear. "Well, what is it?" she asked.

"Oh, it's that stuff about the pickets," Jill replied. "Our home-room teacher told us not to fret too much about it. 'The confrontation of the races,' he called it, that's our burden to bear. Someone, one of the kids, asked him what he meant. He said it was all our faults or our parents' because all of us are so prejudiced. So we would have to take it as our punishment. It upset all of us."

I should think it would, Katie thought. *They* again. Why should *they* make our children feel guilty? I'll bet that teacher said it with a smile, too.

Vowing to do something about it (but knowing she wouldn't), Katie took Jill home and began preparing dinner. Before 5:00 she was interrupted by two telephone calls, one from a friend whom she had known from college and with whom she spoke on a narrow level once a month. The other was from her cousin Katie, her namesake and closest relative. But cousin Katie, a vociferous talker and complainer, was a chore.

Today it was more than she could handle, so Katie Harmon spoke rather curtly to cousin Katie: "Katie, you know, you like to bitch too much. Something—I don't know what—has got to be right."

"Oh, I'm sorry if you think I'm a complainer," said cousin Katie. "I'll try not to disturb you in the future."

It was five more minutes before she could be placated.

It was that kind of day. When Jack came home, Katie was almost herself. But when Jack kept pretty much to himself that night, obviously worried about his career, her mood deteriorated. As she fell asleep that night,

Katie heard Jack ask her something through a wool-like consciousness. She didn't hear what it was and she didn't know what she replied. All she remembered was thinking gratefully:

The day was over.

The bombardment on our senses and values by the communicators is deliberate and constant. The thrust—and none will deny it because at least in its commercial aspects it offers its own excuse—is to beat a clear path to the marketplace, hence, to appeal to the masses. But, in the process, by knowledge, instinct and the experience attained through many years of practice, the vast, endless selling and proselytizing effort employs both the technique of the double-bind and the capitalizing on our internal deficits. The upshot of the latter is a strong yearning to ease some specific frustration on the part of all of us.

Strangely enough—or perhaps not so strangely—individuals who are prone to foist themselves and their wills on others also have the same thrust as the corporate and institutional communicators. What is not so strange about this is that individuals are at the heart of institutions, even those seemingly without a heart or brain but a computer feeding an intricate information system. The policy is established by an individual or a team of individuals. So the lunge at our senses and values comes from the same source.

But it is necessary to make one distinction in the interests of clarity. Aside from a multiplicity of demographic and motivational samplings to which both business and government are given, none of the institutional and cor-

porate communicators have undertaken major pyscho-
logical research to establish the weakness, the foibles
and the gaps in the makeup of the individual consumer
in order to deliver the coup de grace. It could be that
such psychic probes on a mass basis are simply the next
step. In the meantime, the capitalizing on double and
opposing messages to the public and on our own personal frustrations stems, as mentioned earlier, from a
combination of knowledge, instinct and experience. It is
a haphazard but nonetheless dangerous game which
has already had some profoundly serious effects on
Americans. By being sensually desensitized, our values
are being eroded and changed in ways that are difficult
for us to perceive at this time. The effects of this process
will be examined in a later chapter.

In the meantime, let's examine some major examples
of the double-bind in communications and also the play
to our deficits.

*Government.* Obviously, the involvement in Vietnam
was a major double-bind. On one hand, the effort began
in the early sixties as a continuation of the Korean involvement, at least from the standpoint of the principle
of containing communism. But in the late sixties, when
it became clear that the American public had wearied
of the fight, the message was divided into two. Communism must be contained but how can we ignore all the
lives lost in the battle, not to mention the bloodbath that
will surely come from our pulling out of South Vietnam? Hard-liners on both sides of the issue spurned
these double, opposing messages, but the vast majority
of Americans couldn't and didn't. That is the beautiful
cruelty of the double-bind—it impales the conscience.

But there were a number of elements of capitalizing on our deficits, too, in the Vietnam situation. Here are those deficits: Americans hate to lose a war. Americans hate communism. Americans are worried about their declining role in the world. Americans do not like to think of all the many billions of dollars in taxes that were eaten up in the Vietnam war. Since Pearl Harbor, Americans have never felt quite secure with Asiatics. And so on.

There were many other examples in government-public relationships. United States world-trade policy is a classic case of double-bind. Imports have already decimated the domestic electronics, footwear, toy and textile industries, but token efforts to control the flow of foreign goods in other fields are being made. Is the government concerned about the loss of American jobs or about the continuance of international relationships? But the situation, too, has its application to our deficits: are we so weak that we have to close the door on our foreign competitors? If so, won't they close the door on us? In either case, what will happen to the American dollar?

It seems scarcely necessary to explain why other principal government-public issues have their double-binds and deficit catering but merely to mention them. Inflation—a sign of prosperity but a drain on our economy, which is it? Taxes—up, up, up; but is it fully necessary to support a vast governmental organization, not to mention a semiwar economy? A large, volunteer armed force—do we need it? But if not, how can we be ready if we should need a striking force? Similarly with the strategic defense services—needed in our tense world;

but does their presence invite a war, or will they cause one by error? And so on and on.

*Business.* Although American business is replete with double-binds and deficit catering, its biggest communications headache is to justify profits, or the degree of profits, while sustaining its claim of social responsibility. More on this will be discussed in subsequent chapters, but suffice it here to mention the opposing messages transmitted by such business issues as ecology and pollution; quality and workmanship (quality-control experts insist that Japan and West Germany have outstripped us in these respects, but pragmatic businessmen will insist that our salvation depends on our ability to mass-produce); service ability (same argument); influence and ethics (why were the ITT–Justice Department shenanigans so effectively hushed up by an administration that found "nothing largely wrong"?); and fair consideration to minorities (the double-bind here, i.e., "We want them, but you know how few have the education and the sense of responsibility we need," is immense). And so on and on.

But if these goings-on were straining the credibility of business in the minds of most Americans, they were soon to be dwarfed by yet a more shocking disclosure.

Equity Funding Corporation of America, a West Coast insurance and mutual-fund giant, had in its zeal gone beyond the realm of purely creative salesmanship. Over several years, it developed, when a conscience-stricken executive finally leaked it, some of its officers had masterminded a scheme to create fictional insurance policies by the thousands and then sell them for cash to other major life insurers. The conspiracy was known—quite unbelievably—by as many as 1,000 employees of the company who covered it up over several years by intimidation, subterfuge, threats of violence and forged computer tapes.

By mid-1973, thousands of stockholders stood to lose about $300 million in Equity Funding stock as a host of government, Wall Street and regional investigations erupted and while as many as one hundred banks and other financial institutions found themselves stuck with two million shares of stock. Equity's principal officers forthwith resigned, the company was hustled into bankruptcy and the formal grand-jury hearings began, all in a matter of a few months.

But what will take considerably longer will be the return of the public confidence in the good faith of business. The Equity Funding scandal had pushed that confidence to the breaking point.

*Culture.* The problem is more complex. A massive double-bind situation exists between the vitality and impact of modern idioms vs. classical and traditional forms. This entails music, dance, literature, art, sculpture. Question: Are we so unhappy, jaded, uncertain in our hopes that anything new goes, or are we so archaic and conservative that the mobility of the new frightens us? The possibilities of personal deficit applications here are almost endless. But there is even a more basic double-bind in the cultural sphere than the conflict between the contemporary or avant-garde and the traditional idioms. Despite the increase in culture enjoyment in the country, the vast majority of Americans are hardly culture prone. Are we basically a materialistic society—reading fewer books, attending fewer concerts than Europeans—or merely yet an immature one?

And so goes the game of double-bind and deficit catering. Someday an enterprising marketer of adult games will put "The Double-Bind Game" on the market, intriguing the multitudes to guess what the opposing messages are. Or perhaps the game will be "Know Your Deficit." Either could be a means of passing an hour happily. As a game. In real life, the pastime is a bitter one and hardly a diversion.

# 7.

## Tying the Knot on the Double-Bind

IF ALL THE communicators and institutions in our society are playing the double-bind game and exploiting our deficits, if a constant deception is at the heart of their behavior toward us, what effect is it all having on us?

It is making us do the wrong things for the wrong reasons because of wrong stimuli. We are buying things we don't need, accepting ideas we don't believe in, using services we don't want and being jarred into behavior and actions foreign to our natures. We are, in short, being manipulated in almost all our activities—like puppets on a string. Moreover, we are willingly putting ourselves into the hands of the puppet masters only because we aren't conscious of the ways in which we are contributing to the manipulations.

Let's try some more examples representing various functions of our contemporary way of life and see how the deception game works through contrived communications of all types:

## CONSUMER PRODUCTS

Despite all the valiant efforts of the consumerists, business is still pushing products of high obsolescent value, unproven quality, unaesthetic appeal and questionable service backup. Prices have risen at least 10 percent annually in most big-ticket items, such as autos, appliances, furniture and many items of clothing. But have quality of workmanship, serviceability and longevity been correspondingly increased? If that is not a fair question—and I think it is —why all the play on style and superficial appearance rather than on technical advance, safety, improved service?

Television commercials show the neighbors oohing and aahing over a flashy new sports car that a "sophisticated" family down the street bought, or the woman next door rushing in to froth over a sharp new refrigerator, washer, dryer or vacuum cleaner. We are now being treated to plugs on the "getaway" ability of high horsepower, but have you bought a new car lately? It has all the same problems of cars bought ten years ago: doors that stick, hoods that open only with difficulty, batteries that go bad prematurely and so on. Is it that we are still so anxious to dazzle our neighbors or that we succumb to the double-bind? If it looks good it has to be good. Or perhaps being a good product isn't enough, it also has to look good. There is scarcely a product on the market for which some sort of double-bind, inadequate or deceptive sales pitch is not being employed. Is the public too dumb to know better? Perhaps uninformed is a better word—naive, too, and gullible. But the result is that everyone is being stuck with items for which he soon develops a disenchantment.

Questions: Do you brush off the sales pitch and insist on comparing quality, power, service, longevity with competitive products? Do you buy quickly to get it over with? Do you test-try anything before you buy it? Do you press the salesman to support any of his claims? Are you a naive and overwilling customer? I suggest you are.

### SERVICES OF ALL KINDS

Much the same sort of cover-up and deception is practiced in financial, travel, life insurance, consulting and most other services. They play to one's fears—fear that you will not have enough for your economic security, that your loved ones will be destitute on your death, that you will go abroad and have no place to stay or be overcharged, that you need the help of an expert whose knowledge and objectivity will solve all your problems. The double-bind is clear: as a nonexpert in most things, you have problems, and the problems can only be solved by an expert—for a fee, of course. But how much do you know about the insurance you have bought? Much of it loses value as the dollar weakens. Have you considered conversion of older policies into nontaxable bonds that offer more security? The assets of insurers are immense, representing a so-called "surplus surplus," because only a small proportion of their funds are needed at any one time to pay obligations to the insured. How are those custodians of your family's funds investing them? Do you obtain a dividend and how does that "yield" on your money compare with the return on stocks, bonds, certificates of deposit, mutual funds and such? And how good are bank investment and money-management services? If truth were known, many of them do no better with the estates entrusted to them than might be done by the private person investing intelligently. But for a fee the money-management service takes that "detail" off your hands. Is that how you want to regard the maintenance of what you've worked for all these years? Shouldn't you pay more attention, involve yourself in the manner in which it is being administered?

Travel agencies provide a service in arranging packaged tours and in making reservations for the traveler, but in many cases reservations are in the higher priced and often less popular hotels. Reason: a better deal for the agent. But the traveler is stuck when he arrives; he can't easily switch. Suggestion: tell your agent that you don't want a fleabag and don't want to pay through the nose. You might well ask which are the best hotels in the area. And, while you're at it, check the arrangements your agent has made on airlines with what you can do on your own.

If you're a businessman, do a bit of checking on the consultant you hire. What's his actual business experience? Ask him to give you a list of his recent clients and check them. Will they automatically endorse him because he cited them? Maybe not. Watch out for the theoretical consultant. Ask him for some account of previous recommendations he has made elsewhere and from that you may get some feeler as to his pragmatism.

In other words, when it comes to services of any kind and you feel a need for them, often justifiable, don't let your own fears, your own sense of insecurity, turn you into a gullible, pliant customer. Assert yourself—you may become undeceived in the process—and still obtain the service you want.

### POLITICS

For some reason that may be purely indigenous to Americans, we have accepted the principles of the double-bind, the playing to our frustrations (or deficits), and deception in connection with politics and government as though they were essential traits of those two related functions of our society. If politics refers to shrewdness and sagacity in promoting governmental policy, it is difficult to see where politics ends and government begins. Are our presidents, their cabinets and most principal politicians manipulators of the public consciousness? If the average American were asked this question, he would probably agree and, furthermore, accept the fact that his leaders must perform their roles in a devious, mastermind manner if they are to succeed in our checks-and-balances, hurly-burly system of democracy.

© 117

Power in the nation's capital can be drawn graphically in the shape of a triangle, the three prime angles being the executive, congressional and regulatory branches. At the triangle's center is a pressure area, which causes a distortion of the triangle when the stress reaches a severe point. And that distortion has in five recent national administrations been on the side of the President and has been caused by a combination of his manipulative skills and personality. Here's the way those five administrations might look in the form of a triangle and its variations:

## THE SHAPE OF NATIONAL POWER

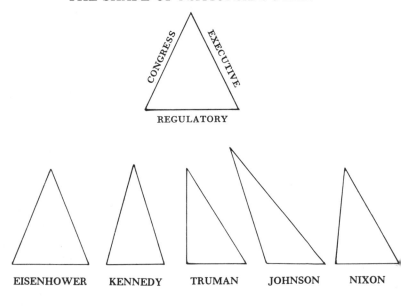

*A* (equilateral): *Bland Presence*—Gen. Dwight D. Eisenhower, whose tenure was marked by dullness and status quo, except for the High Court decision on minority rights.

B (isosceles): *Bright, Dazzling Presence*—John F. Kennedy, 1,000 days of the Beautiful People, a confrontation with the Russians in Cuba and an inability to cope with Congress, a tough bunch to dazzle.

C (right-angled): *Hard-Rock Presence*—Harry S. Truman, whose flinty steadfastness and conviction moved Congress and the world but flicked many a skin.

D (obtuse): *Too-Grating Presence*—Lyndon B. Johnson, whose image making finally outwitted him and alienated his friends in Congress. But for a while, it was a one-man government.

E (scalene): *The All-Presence*—Richard M. Nixon, his preeminent powers as an image maker and manipulator often outwitted Congress and stalemated the agencies.

As a newspaperman who has spent an increasing amount of time in Washington, I have come to conclude from both personal observations and numerous interviews that there are many double-binds practiced in the capital but that only one predominates. It is simply that in the seat of national decision, most decisions are not made in the national interest but to satisfy regional or specialized pressures. Yet many of these are purported to be national in importance. And the average citizen is often lulled into that belief because of the glib and persuasive manner with which many politicians rationalize their convictions. The opposing messages beamed out in the double-bind process are, "If you want to clean the rivers and the air, beautify the countryside and stem the urban blight, it must begin on a regional basis or, since the problem is regional in nature, it will never mean anything to us as a nation." So we accept this blindly, few of us having taken the time or trouble or, for that matter, having the opportunity to investigate the matter.

In the process, local constituents are pleased, particularly when their national representatives in the Senate, the House or "friends" at the White House or the regulatory agencies have the proper amount of influence to achieve their specialized demands. But others, whose advocates haven't, are disappointed.

Why, for example, did Washington bail out the Lockheed Corporation when it ran into financial difficulties with a balky jet engine, but not Boeing, whose problems represented another regional situation? And why did the solons who claim a national conscience refuse to extend a financial lifeline to bankrupt Penn Central when that depressed national rail line desperately needed it? My argument is not intended to support the principle that government must run to the help of business when its highly paid management falls flat but to underscore the point that specialized interests frequently win out over other specialized interests and particularly over the national interest.

"The business of this town is for everyone here representing someone else to make a position for himself," declared Robert C. Farrow of the Washington staff of Carl Byoir & Co., one of the country's leading public-relations agencies. A specialist in government information and relations and a former administrative assistant to Congressman D. S. Saund of southern California, Farrow added, "But so much is happening simultaneously that is difficult for anyone to compete and make a big impact. So everyone looks for a telling angle."

Congressmen who like to refute the claim that they indulge in image making do a considerable amount of it in order to get reelected, said Farrow. "Congressmen are mostly returned to Washington for what they do for their constituents and are constantly engaged in soliciting letters from them so that they can do something for the home folks and have something to show on the record," he said. "Senators, who are more nationally minded because they represent their state rather than a community within it, have an even greater problem—they, too, have to show local accomplishments in order to push for reelection. It's not a simple situation."

No doubt about it. But if persuasion, deception and double-binds are needed to obtain one's rights in the nation's capital (and in the state capitals, as well), the fact is that the trend toward manipulating for special interests is booming in Washington. Within the last five years, lobbying organizations have mushroomed. These can range from a one-man outfit operating from a single desk and telephone in a multipartitioned office to large staffs occupying entire floors or buildings. Most recently, the activity has led to the founding of "The Center for ——" for whatever special interests want to proselytize. There are more than one hundred of these in Washington, representing reporting services anxious to relay specialized information to particular groups of one kind or another, specialized interests wanting to know what is going on in the power crucible. And at least some of these "Centers" do not mind slanting either their reporting or their information-disseminating services. The result of the proliferation of reporting services for special interests willing to pay for them can, at the very least, mean additional mitigation against the interests of the average American.

## ENTERTAINMENT

Within a heady three weeks between March 15 and April 5, 1966, three major American magazines, *Life, Look* and *Vogue,* devoted their covers to an odd-looking, long-nosed and cat-eyed girl with a boyish bob. Thanks to the push of her publicists, Solters, O'Rourke & Sabinson, and to what they called her "unerring instinct" for knowing what's right or wrong, Barbra Streisand, a singer whose loud, wailing voice had delighted or outraged Broadway movie audiences and television viewers, had wrought a near-miracle.

On two covers, those of *Life* and *Look,* the insecurity and implicit sadness of the singer were blurbed. "Barbra Streisand, the fear-ridden girl behind the star," proclaimed *Life.* "Barbra Streisand, the not-so-funny story of that Funny Girl," promoted *Look.* Contrasted with this sympathetic promise was *Vogue*'s cover with its Streisand photo: "Barbra Streisand at the Paris Collections." The large *Vogue* picture of Streisand added whimsy to its pitch: she had a large orchid protruding from her mouth.

Which was the real Streisand, the fear-ridden, not-so-funny one or the one parading through the Paris couture sucking on an orchid? Did it matter? Did anyone care? The magazines did and so, one must assume, did the singer and her publicists. And without question, the public did, too.

But the question is, why? If, as is patently the case, we are interested in the human being behind the celebrity and the artist, why is a deception practiced on the un-suspecting public? If Miss Streisand can be fear-ridden and not-so-funny in almost successive weeks, can she change her personality enough in virtually the same week as to prance through fashion shows with an or-chid coming out of her mouth? Rather than make a specious thing of merely a few covers on which Strei-sand was featured (she was on others, too), my point is that, obviously, in the case of the *Life, Look* and *Vogue* covers and their articles, an image maker was at work to cast his client in the kind of palatable image that the public would swallow. Was Lee Solters aware of the sharp contrast in his client's personality as portrayed on the three covers? Not at all. Solters, a veteran publicist with thirty-seven years in the entertainment and cul-tural field, could only rave about the girl and what he had done for her.

"That instinct of hers," he told me, "the image of a nightclub singer was always that of a beautiful girl in a beautiful gown. But she knew she had to be different. So when she started singing, she came out in one night-club wearing a gingham dress. The audience was im-mediately put off. And when she finished her first song, they went wild. They stamped their feet. They banged on their glasses. Truman Capote was in the audience and he yelled, 'She's beautiful!' "

Why are we being put on by the image makers of

© 123

entertainers, performing artists and others who appeal either to our emotions or our aesthetic senses or to both? "For maximum appeal" is the surface answer, but it falls into the province of a double-bind as well. If we are attracted by the art of the performer, what do we stand to lose by not knowing him or her as a human being, too? Why should we care, anyway? But the image makers and the artists themselves sense that every one in the unwashed public would enjoy seeing the artist step down off the pedestal and show his feet of clay.

Why is that? Are we so anxious to cut the celebrity down to life size that we (1) don't feel like the peasant in the pit looking up at the idol on the stage; (2) enjoy the performance better knowing that the performer has the same family problems, generation gap, insecurity and hangups that we do? Or, put another way, is it an appeal to our own deficit of a lack of identity and sense of inferiority?

And so we are treated to family portraits—the artist at home in sloppy bedroom shoes, warts and all—of Frank Sinatra, Bing Crosby, Danny Thomas, Lucille Ball, Mia Farrow, Liza Minnelli, Leonard Bernstein, et al.

Sinatra, who retired as America's most important pop singer in 1971 after ruling the TV, jukebox and record circuits for three decades, is generally considered even by serious musicologists as one of the major singers in American music of the twentieth century. He was also a master of the image-making techniques that raised artists and entertainers on the American scene to heights of stunning popularity and wealth, such as Caruso, Pons, Bob Hope, Jackie Gleason, Streisand, Johnny Carson, Johnny Cash, Sid Caesar and, more recently, Sonny and Cher.

In Sinatra's case, the image-making ability came from natural sources, a skill at singing to the listener, especially those young girls in the forties to whom Sinatra's way of phrasing more for the meaning than for the musical shape registered intimately. It came also from a long use of public-relations practitioners who helped him to perpetuate a career for years, first as a wispy young man whose soft eyes and lyrical voice were fixed on something beyond the hysteria and materialism of the age and then as a senior singer whose voice and appeal refused to age along with his body. Even when he ran into unfavorable publicity, Sinatra's image didn't suffer long. Like that of Bing Crosby (their careers paralleled in many ways), Sinatra remained a well-loved and respected entertainer-turned-entrepreneur.

What is it in our national penchant for hero worship that raises an unquestionably successful star to the rank of "superstar"? Henry Hewes, the drama critic of the *Saturday Review,* had some potent thoughts on the question in his 1971 review of the highly popular musical *Jesus Christ Superstar:*

> In the beginning is the word and the word is "superstar." Presumably, it originated in Hollywood and is part of the whole overblown phony process in which the distinctions between talent and the willingness to become an enormously popular symbol have been wiped out. Laurence Olivier and John Gielgud are generally considered to be two of the world's greatest actors, but no one alludes to them as superstars. The Hollywood creation of superstars is, in fact, a base, illusory process that panders to the need of people to worship something that is, on the surface at least, infinitely larger and more dazzling than themselves.

> The most insidious aspect of this process is that it tends to subvert whatever talent the star originally possessed.

What propelled *Jesus Christ Superstar* to emerge as a superstar musical? Before the Broadway version even opened, MCA, Inc., the entertainment complex, netted $16.5 million on record albums and tapes. An eight-week tour of a singing troupe took in more than $2 million. The sponsors soon projected that *Superstar* would be the biggest concert-grossing event of all times. The Broadway presentation was a smash and a film production was quickly set.

The *Superstar* entrepreneurs simply claimed that timing, subject and presentation were in the right juxtaposition. But a vast publicity campaign helped, too, feeding on the combination of rock music, a new focus on religion (especially among young people) and something else. This last factor was the impact of the incongruity, somewhat akin to *Fiddler on the Roof* being played in West Germany or *Gone With the Wind* in Japan. Placing Jesus in a circuslike, rock-music revivalist environment intrigued the public who saw it and sent patrons away with a fervor caused by the humanization of Jesus.

How much impact is due to illusion and how much to true entertainment? Does a singer who sports a sequined jacket, luminous pants and long hair tied by a ribbon at his nape provide additional impact or illusion to his performance? Does a symphony conductor who bobs, weaves and seemingly self-flagellates when he conducts enhance the music? The answer is simple. We, the audience, welcome the illusion. It becomes part of the entertainment, and we love it dearly even when we know that it is unreal, false and, yes, illusion.

And, of course, we the public also savor the celebrity unmasked, the glamorous star seen in her rumpled nightie minus makeup (or seemingly so). We allow ourselves to be convinced, or at least impressed, by the entertainer turned commercial pitchman. But that effort to convince, either in the nightie or in the commercial, is a put-on, part of an unending roll of salami fed to us slice by slice and often full of just plain sawdust. And sometimes, as in the case of Streisand on three magazine covers in less than a month, the image even breaks apart through pure overkill.

Is there anything substantive in the so-called "star" quality? It's a little hard to believe it in these days when the blurbs on Broadway, the movies and television hail every new face with the magnetism that excites audiences. A new star has arrived—make way, in other words. But these evidences of deceptive hoopla aside, even a cynic must admit that a performer occasionally comes along whose rapport with the audience is real and lasting. In the field of popular entertainment, those who truly had that aura were Judy Garland, Barbra Streisand, the Beatles, Richard and Elizabeth Burton, Sinatra, and Carol Channing. In the concert field, it's difficult to think of any who had it more than Enrico Caruso, Lily Pons, Leonard Bernstein and Arthur Rubinstein.

Does Luciano Pavarotti, the grinning, 300-pound new lyric tenor, the new "golden voice" of the Metropolitan Opera, have it? So we're being told.

And "being told" is an important part of the audience's consciousness. Publicists claim that it isn't possible to foist an untalented performer on the public and manipulate that performer into artist and even star quality. "You can sell a Ford," says Harvey Sabinson, one of New York's best-known Broadway publicists, "but not an Edsel."

But how many times have we been told that so-and-so is another Caruso or Bjoerling, that that dancer is another Astaire or Gene Kelly or Pavlova, that that movie actor who displays virility, has big ears and talks out of the other side of his mouth is another Bogey or Gable? So whatever happened to David Janssen, Rock Hudson, Stephen Boyd, Richard Crenna?

Perhaps Mr. Sabinson is right, but the prolonged blasts of hot air the entertainment world gives us, the immense advertisements and endless billboards and commercials have probably caused more people to plunk down hard cash for inflated movie and theater prices than were justified by the doubtful talents of many "stars" or questionable content of numerous new "hits."

What of the Burtons, that dramatic couple who seem to bestride the international movie scene like no others? Do they have publicity-and-advertising minions? After all, if you were to list those couples who command more space and attention than any others, it is probable that even the Nixons, Queen Elizabeth and Prince Philip, Princess Grace and Prince Rainier, Ari and Jacqueline Onassis receive no more and maybe even less than the Burtons.

According to John Springer, the publicity man who

handles the Burtons, his biggest trouble is to keep them away from the press. So what happened when Elizabeth contracted measles while making a movie in Cortina, Italy, and stories proliferated in the world's press like a runaway rash of the disease itself? And then proliferated again when Richard, too (naturally), was quarantined? Explains Springer, with the kind of easy smile that might disarm many, "Everything the Burtons do makes news."

Maybe.

True, on some nights when you twirl the channel selector, you may if you are lucky achieve the ultimate—three or four movies in which the former Elizabeth Taylor is twelve years old on one channel (*National Velvet*), eighteen years old on another, twenty-four years old on a third and thirty-five or more on the last channel. She has been around on the public consciousness for a long time. And, to be honest about it, forget the fits of temperament, the marital problems of the past and the occasional spats with Richard of more recent vintage, she remains a very interesting child-girl-woman-vamp whose real-life carrying-on often becomes inseparable from her varied roles in the movies.

Charisma? No doubt about it. "Look," insists Springer, "she's still one of the most beautiful women in the world and Burton is generally considered one of the finest actors in the English-speaking world. Both have that indefinable quality of excitement, glamour and talent—and maybe that trait of independence—that attracts the public to the entertainment media when they are on and even outside it. They never seek publicity, they rarely grant interviews, and except for some occasional stories that Elizabeth may want when she gets a new jewel or a yacht, they don't want to be in the press."

Those occasional stories that Elizabeth Burton seeks, Springer says, involve some new possession that she is inordinately proud of, somewhat "like a little girl." But what the Burtons are adamantly against is publicity on their philanthropic endeavors, which Springer calls "considerable." Why is that? asks the ever-cynical reporter. "Elizabeth insists—and Richard agrees with her —that if she has to earn a good image with the public by broadcasting their charity contributions, then they don't want to be liked."

Besides, says Springer, being perhaps more practical, "publicizing those contributions would just make them sitting ducks for pleas for every real and fake need all over the world."

Carol Channing, now crowding sixty, has also been a crowd-pleaser from the time she appeared in a not-too-well remembered Broadway revue, *Lend An Ear*. Her high rasping voice, big, rolling eyes, good legs and come-hither look made her stand out, and she has been on the top of the Broadway-television scene ever since that show of 1948 vintage. Sabinson handles her publicity needs and also claims that she doesn't need much help. "I don't know anyone today who has the kind of audience rapport that she does. She remained the star of *Hello, Dolly* as long as she wanted to and continues in great demand."

Thus, the question of "star" quality and the need or lack of it for a star's publicity. Probably the answer is that if an entertainer or performer of any kind has talent in a big dose, publicity isn't as important as that needed for a performer whose talent is of a lesser degree. No one will quarrel or carp with the value of publicity and promotion as an informational device—but we can rail at and resent the type of publicity-promotion blasts that seek to deceive and part us from our money and attract an even more valuable commodity, our time and attention.

In pursuit of my research, I spoke to a number of psychiatrists and sociologists on how the communications deception is maintained and what it is doing to us. I repeat a cross section of their remarks, largely informal and chatty, which is the way the discussions went, and without any attribution, which is what most if not all of them preferred.

> We live largely and increasingly for appearance, what the outside thinks of us. We buy a particular kind of car. We are a little bit more upper than lower in this respect. There are certain kinds of people who will drive only a Mercedes Benz and there are people who are perfectly willing to drive a Chevrolet all their lives. These are an expression of the standards by which we judge each other, but they are external values and they have nothing to do with what we are as people, what we have as inner potentials as human beings. And each one of us is biologically different, that's the marvelous thing about biology.
>
> What does the habit of people wanting to live by external things do to them? They run the danger of losing diversity and it's only in diversity that you gain important qualities. By being different one from the other you achieve competition, stimulation, differentiation, varieties of ideas and developments which are unforeseeable.

So when people live by external things, they really reduce their own individuality. If you live in Fairmount or Fair Lawn, a lot of your attitude or values will be governed by the fact that you have four or five or ten neighbors who have houses that cost pretty much what yours did and they go to Sears, Roebuck and buy a particular kind of thing and you have human beings who are stamped out in the Fairmount or Fair Lawn or other stamp and they are Sears, Roebuck kind of people.

We develop concepts or slogans and then for a while our whole cultural pattern follows them. The Vietnamese war and our involvement in it is classical by now. As the concept evolved, there were all the liberals in Washington during the Kennedy Administration who perpetuated the great myth that we had to resist communism and this became a basic premise for everyone. This notion hadn't been seriously thought through for perhaps twenty-five years and this one premise was thrown at us as a principle for which we should get in and stay in the war. It was a slogan that wasn't reappraised for years until only recently.

What about the Edsel and the midi, two propositions that the public turned down squarely—didn't these show that the public will be undeceived when it wishes? Replied one sociologist:

Such things are individual events which for a particular reason don't follow the pattern. The notion of women wearing a certain kind of dress had been pretty well fixed and the extreme change apparently was such as to provoke a highly negative response. The downfall of the Edsel arose from the fact that its introduction came at a bad moment when the car market was weak, feeble, compacts were coming in strongly and the big new car couldn't take off.

One psychologist saw the matter in a different light, citing the "theory of waste," a natural phenomenon which stretched its influence over men and matters. And the survival of the fittest applied to both men and matters. He said:

> From biology through every scientific discipline, there is always a kind of waste, every species overdevelops. The number of human sperm can make ten million babies with every act of intercourse. And yet all but a few sperm go to waste. It is because, as Darwinian thinking insists, nature always provides more than it needs to sustain a particular system. I think this concept holds true in every area of living.
>
> In every family with a large number of children, there are some who are waste products. They are the ne'er-do-wells. In the Middle Ages, families with too many girls sent them to convents because they didn't know what to do with them. They had no role, no place. There are women who fall by the wayside and there are Edsels that fall by the wayside. In a play by Tennessee Williams, *The Night of the Iguana*, there is a story of the lizards who came from thousands of eggs laid in the sand. The eggs matured and all the lizards had to do to survive was move from the sand to the more solid earth, perhaps fifty feet, but the birds were ready to pounce. That was part of nature's ecology. Only a very small number survived. These were just the strongest, the toughest and the fastest. And, in a great sense, human society is not that different. You have the Bowery bums, the welfare-nicks, the people who never make it in society, the retardees, the people who are bio-

logically deficient in some way. In terms of human evolution they are basically waste products.

He continued,

Our so-called democratic society doesn't permit us to look at it this way but if you were up there looking down on us, say, the same distance from humanity as from earth to the stars, you would see that this is stardust, fall-off, throw-off. It's not necessary unless it has the qualities to survive, only the things that meet the needs of the time do survive. It is inhuman indeed, but not to perceive it and to pretend that it isn't so is simply a lack of understanding and perhaps a lack of communication. . . . Take a large, impoverished family with nine or ten children, legitimate and illegitimate. You know that most of them are going to fall by the wayside. You cannot rescue them. I have tried. I really have. Because a human being costs money. Basically, it's not only the love you give a child but the money you put into him—the kind of school, the kind of skills and training, the time that parents spend with them, the kind of food they eat, the place they live in, the amount of leisure, the amount of opportunity for both physical and social skills.

All this is money. This is all reducible to economic terms. If you want to produce a quality product, human or otherwise, it's like producing a good suit of clothes. You have to put an awful lot of good stuff in a suit to produce a good one and you have to put a lot into a child to make a quality child. And even then you are not guaranteeing a quality child, but without it you are certainly guaranteeing a nonquality child.

Observed a demographic expert:

Why does the public sometimes reject an idea, a product, a service that is proposed to it with a great fanfare of advertising and publicity? If you create a certain milieu in the idea or product marketplace, it cannot function simply by the turning on of a switch. In other words, you can't turn it on instantaneously. If you feed the public something suddenly that is too far out, that is substantially inconsistent with their preconditioning, they'll reject it. The whole commercial syndrome has a certain profile as does the cultural syndrome, a certain character at any given time. Now precisely because it is so rigid, if you try to change it abruptly, people are going to reject it. It has to be done slowly.

If you try to convince every woman that she ought to have perfume, you can't a week later pitch her successfully on the fact that the natural smell of a woman is far more attractive than the unreal, plastic scents of perfume. You could eventually bring them around to that, you could eventually bring the female to rejecting perfume. But you can't make her reject it from Monday to Thursday.

A woman psychologist was asked what she thought about the aggressive push on feminine-hygiene deodorants. Does the whole message represent a double-bind? She said:

I think it is a beautiful example of double-binding in our society. Because everything in advertising says be more feminine, be more sexy, be what a man wants. Everything in advertising seems to aim at producing a sexual image of the female. Then some advertiser introduces a product that says, in effect, that if you really mean to have sex, then you must let the smell out. Because sex smells, that's the truth. So they say now be sexy but cover up the smell. Not that most women smell. They bathe every day. But regardless, the sponsor says be nice, be sexy, but don't stink. That is really the message underneath the cute, bland commercial, and it is such a double-binding thing because it tells two opposite things. And it's devastating to a woman. It truly splits her personality. The more sexy she gets, the more she oozes; the more she has sexual feelings, the more her natural juices come out. This is what you're supposed to wash away or destroy by using the new deodorant product. In one way, they're saying be sexy but if you're really sexy (and thus human) you stink. They're really opposing messages.

I asked the woman psychologist and later a male sociologist what they thought of the National Airlines' "I'm Barbara . . . Fly Me" campaign. Said the woman psychologist:

Just the term 'Fly Me' has such a clearly sexual connotation that it wouldn't surprise me if it became another word for having sex. I mean if kids pick it up and say, "Fly Me," it wouldn't greatly surprise me. This is the way language evolves. When I first heard the term, it shocked me and I'm not a very shockable person. But to be this blatant really got to me.

The male sociologist said that he found the "Fly Me" campaign objectionable

because it is a little bit like dirty-boy sex. There's a whole world of obscenity in an expression that makes everyone giggle. If you say "fuck," everyone know what it means. At least, good, healthy run-of-the-mill obscenity is honest, but this is dirty-boy sex. It reminds me of when I was just out of high school and trying to make some money to get to college. I worked in a shoe store summers and the great big joke was when one salesman would yell down to another salesman, "Get me a size nine rubbers." Everyone would laugh, thinking of condoms. Well, this is in the same category, using a sort of dirty word but not using a real dirty word but a kind of salesman's humor.

### Foisting the Fantasy as Reality

A psychiatrist had this to say:

One of the salient features about advertising that I have noticed is that the more the advertiser identifies a product with sexuality, the more attractive he makes it. In other words—SEXIFY EVERYTHING. Sexify cars, planes, refrigerators, shaving cream, deodorants, little cigars—everything. The only thing that they don't sexify is detergents, which they put on to men. Do you realize how many men advertise detergents? Take Mr. Clean, for one example. For another, the guy who always carries one very famous brand of detergent is a man. Personally, I think that women hate housework so much that this may be why they demasculinize men on television. Maybe it's that simple—the advertising agencies know that women really loathe anything to do with washing, cleaning and so on.

But if a man is selling a particular detergent and putting the clothes into a machine, my image of him is that he is a passive little boy. Even in this day and age when men are still supposed to be masculine, it is difficult to swallow the idea of men running around all the time to do the family wash. There is this problem that faces advertisers. How can you sell a product to a woman who hates the use that it has to be put to? And so we are being treated to quite a number of tiny, dumpy, even very feminine little men going down to the apartment-house laundry room.

# III.

# The Communicators and the Press

# 8.

## Advertising—
## Parity and
## Peter Pan

### THE CONSTANT DILEMMA

SMARTING from a mushroom cloud of consumerists' criticisms and crackdowns on advertising claims by the Federal Trade Commission, major consumer-goods makers only partly turned the other cheek in the late 1960s and early '70s. The result of much of it was a pasty mélange of ineffective sales pitch and inoffensive claims. Naturally from both the sales and credibility standpoints, it had the clout of a marshmallow hurled at a daisy in a fifty-mile-an-hour wind.

How to sell, creatively stimulate and still not offend by deceiving?

Wonder Bread, while temporarily deterred from banging away that its product "builds strong bodies 12 ways," adopted a cutesy but less ambitious pitch. Loaves, known as "Fresh Guys," plopped out of stoves and deported themselves in animated antics. Profile Bread was touted as a diet loaf but its only real contribution to weight reduction was thinner slices. So, in a corrective ad, actress Julia Meade pleasantly admitted, "But eating Profile will not cause you to lose weight." And Geritol, no longer allowed to claim that it was just the thing for tired blood, shifted to celebrities familiar to the Geritol generation who proclaimed, "I *feel better* because I take Geritol."

Different, but not very, in principle was Ford Motor Company's radio-television pitch in between product recalls on more than 140,000 Torinos and 900,000 cars and trucks. The pitch was: "Listening Better. Building Better. That's Ford!" Chrysler Corporation's message was a bit more subtle: "Visit your Chrysler-Plymouth dealer. He wants to sell you peace of mind. So CALM DOWN!" Why not? Automobile prices did go up annually, despite price controls.

In recent years, the gray pains of parity and the traumatic and financial pangs that accompany both governmental and society censure have saddled leading advertisers and their agencies with many of their most anxious moments in decades. So great has been the pressure and stigma inflicted on Madison Avenue and its clients in the last five years that the constant problem of devising ways with which to make a hundred million American consumers part with their dollars has become a tortured process. In it, the most common solution has been a return to dull, often stupid advertising commonplaces. Gone are the creative sixties—welcome to the dumb seventies.

What brought the advertising business to this sad stage? The largest American service industry, the advertising field, accounts for an expenditure of an estimated $20 billion annually or roughly 2 percent of the country's gross national product. With that degree of financial impact on the nation's mass media, what is the urgency for deception? Only the competition that exists in the marketplace. It is a competition that has grown sharply over the years but which still fails to avoid the reality of parity in many products. It may come as a shock to those who prefer to wear rose-colored glasses, but many products made in America for mass use reflect parity, the state of being equal in virtually every aspect with other products.

The color, trim or detail, packaging, labeling and other inconsequentials may be different but there is scarcely a difference in ingredients in many brands of toothpaste, detergents and soaps, packaged foods, electronics, automobiles, beer, cigarettes and tobacco, ad infinitum. So how can the advertiser increase market share, consumer loyalty, market penetration, shelf space at retail and so forth, when his beloved product isn't markedly different from another's beloved product? By a preemptive claim, of course. The only rub is that the preemptive claim, the claim that literally lifts a product above and beyond the qualifications of any similar products on the market, is no longer allowed on parity products by the watch-dogging FTC. Thus, a part of the dilemma is the increasing stringency of governmental policing of advertising practices.

But the advertiser's dilemma has at least two more elements.

One is the client-agency relationship, a rapport represented by a fine skein which is rapidly being torn asunder by the onslaught of jabs from both the public and private sectors. The other is the loss of public credibility in the advertising effort, one of the most disturbing aspects in the entire picture.

So these are the three components of today's dilemma in the advertising business and they are also its three main causes.

But what *really* brought Madison Avenue—and its counterparts elsewhere in other major American cities —to its knees? I suggest that it is the advertising community's Peter Pan syndrome. You know Peter Pan. He was the pixyish boy in the James Barrie play of that name who never grew up. He exists; he lives today on Madison Avenue and among its clients. Advertising never really grew up or seemingly wanted to. Perhaps it is because, in our classic American hard-selling push, no one will let it.

### PARITY IN ACTION

Copywriters in anguish, advertisers in a sweat, media beefing up their acceptability staffs and the government and even advertising policing boards studying each ad, monitoring each commercial in a tizzy of concentration. Is that the situation on Madison Avenue these days? Just about.

So project this scene:

# The Communicators and the Press

[*A big advertiser (to be known as* B.A.*) is meeting with the representatives of his advertising agency, namely the account supervisor* (A.S.) *and the copywriter* (COPY) *to draft a new campaign on a food product. The advertising pitch on the product has come under* FTC *censure and additionally its sales have slipped badly.*]

THE B.A.: What we desperately need, gentlemen, is a message, a theme, that will avoid bringing Washington down on our heads again but will increase our tonnage and bring us back to where we were five years ago.

A.S.: Fine, George, we fully understand this and we've already done some preliminary work. The problem, though, is complex as all hell—how to avoid a preemptive claim and at the same time create a dominant identity minus any claim of supremacy.

B.A.: But, dammit, the product is the best in the field. We've tested it out and the results came back affirmatively. Why can't we say so?

A.S.: You can't unless you can produce undisputed documentary proof that it is the best, the unique product. Can you do that, George?

B.A.: Well, we used to say, "Treat yourself to the best—you deserve it!" And then they made us stop using that. Gentlemen, I'll be utterly candid with you, our product is no different from three others on the market but what we have going for us is that we were the first and we used to be the biggest seller. I still say we've got the best franchise with the public and all we have to do is to capitalize on that franchise—to get that loyalty back in actual numbers.

[*Silence reigns for a few moments until the short, fat, bearded copywriter bestirs himself. He bangs a massive pipe against an ash tray and holds up a sheet of paper.*]

COPY: We put together a couple of ideas or three. You see, your product was pitched to an audience of all ages but the biggest sales component was accounted for by kids who liked it for breakfast. Now, if we can get across the idea that adults need at least as much energy as kids in this youthful world—

B.A.: Nope, that's too radical a shift. The backup costs, use of new media, packaging, point-of-sale displays and so on—it would be too much. Besides, one of the other packagers has that market sewed up. The whole effort would be prohibitive. Got anything else?

A.S. *(a bit grimly):* We sure have, George.

COPY: All right, now how about this? A play on fast acceleration, like Detroit pushes. Our breakfast food is an instant starter—put it in your tank and away you go! We don't have any copy yet but I visualize the kind of graphics that shows a kid, a college girl or an adult catapulting out of their chairs—

B.A. *(thoughtfully):* Well, it's a steal from a couple of other campaigns and frankly I'm not so sure it will pass muster. They're asking everyone nowadays to substantiate their claims—but maybe. I don't know. Got anything else?

This scene is fictional, of course, but it is not very remote from many an actual situation. The hot breath of a number of federal agencies such as the Federal Trade Commission, the Federal Communications Commission and the Food and Drug Administration has changed the rules on Madison Avenue as has the simultaneous push by consumer advocates such as Ralph Nader. The thrust of governmental policing increased in 1972 in a number of ways. One of them was demonstrated between June and September when the FTC asked twenty-eight manufacturers and advertisers of soap and detergent products to submit documentation for certain advertising claims in sixty days. Among the claims were:

Mr. Bubble cleans effectively and does not leave bathtub rings.

Purex gets dirt other bleaches leave behind.

Lifebuoy is so lastingly active, its deodorant protection won't let you down.

Dial is used by many hospitals to bathe newborn babies and is the most effective deodorant soap on the market.

Clothes that are so dirty they appear to be ruined can be effectively cleaned and restored by washing them in Tide.

In issuing the orders, the FTC said it was not filing complaints against the companies for any violations but was merely gathering information to determine what substantiation exists to support major advertising claims. By doing so, the agency explained, it could better evaluate competing claims and ascertain who was advertising truthfully.

But sometimes the contortions that advertisers and their agencies are undergoing in the wake of the government's push and the critical barrage lead to a greater immorality than was perpetrated in the original, deceptive theme. That greater immorality may involve an undue influence on an unsophisticated segment of the public by paid testimonials by respected public figures; unfounded factual or hypoed ethnic references; or exaggerations that are not as much patently deceptive as generalized and vague. Within the advertising community, many an agency is watching its competitors closely to seize on such questionable recoveries from a dishonest campaign.

The answer to the prohibition of the preemptive claim, of course, is for novel, creative executions. In an industry partially paralyzed by a mass of censure, it is still possible to find recent instances of creative responses to the challenge of parity or near-parity situations.

Doyle Dane Bernbach, which, according to *Advertising Age,* is "widely believed to be the world's most creative agency," had a problem not too long ago involving parity products. In this case, the product was a television set and Sylvania TV was the client. Here was the situation, the rationale and the conclusion as related in an interview with Leon Meadow, DDB's vice-president, creative management supervisor and head of the copy department:

> In connection with the restrictions today, what does an agency do about parity products where you have a product with no more advantages or disadvantages than another fellow's product and yet your job is to sell your product against his product? DDB handles it one way, BBDO handles it another and Ted Bates a third way. We do it by sticking strictly within the perimeters set down by our legal counsel and working from that as a base. DDB relies on its creative strengths to come out with the most believable statements that can be made about the product and there is language that you can use to convince a person. You tell the truth and you do it disarmingly. Perhaps in some cases you are self-deprecating or at least humorous or say that my product won't solve all the problems in the world. It

was manufactured to do this little job and it does it very nicely.

It is that kind of attitude which, in the face of the lack of superiority claims, at least gets across to the average consumer at one point or another the idea that this guy is not out to take me. That he is taking a stance that is more moderate and is perhaps more believable than the next guy.

I think a good example of such a situation in a parity product is a TV set. RCA, Zenith, Motorola, and Sylvania (our client) all put out good sets, they all give you, relatively speaking, good values for the money. As soon as one comes out with a gadget of some kind, his competitor will have it that same season or at the latest on the next go-round.

So what do you do? You rack your brains and you say how can I present this story creditably and memorably and still stay within the FTC bounds. What we did in this shop was create a commercial in which we dropped all reference to automatic color control, instant-on picture, 100 percent solid state and the rest of the so-called features that go into the selling of a TV set. We said, let's make a demonstration that is memorable and hope that a fellow will go into a store and say, hey, I saw that commercial on television and can you tell me if that set is as good as they say it is on TV? And so we did a commercial that is called "The Cat and the Canary."

It opens with a cat framed in a windowsill, an open window, and he looks into the window and stops. We cut to a canary fluttering around in a cage. Then we cut back to the cat. His eyes widen in what is obviously relish and the cat jumps through the window and drops to the floor. We cut back and forth in between the cat and the bird fluttering. Finally, the stalking cat stops, snarls and

© 149

springs. As he springs, the camera pulls back and you see that the canary in the cage is really on TV and the cat has sprung at the TV set and is scratching at the glass. End of commercial.

That commercial has been the subject of a tremendous amount of talk in the industry and in the advertising business, very favorable, although there was a lot of letters from cat lovers saying that cats don't do that. The client loved it, obviously. It didn't sell a damn thing really, except that it has this beautiful memorability. After the concept was created, we spent the next two months with lawyers, ours and the client's lawyers and then with network lawyers in setting up a regimen of procedure that would allow us to do the commercial.

How do we satisfy all these lawyers? The first question came on the matter of copy. We could not obviously call this a demonstration because it wasn't a demonstration. It was more technically and more correctly a dramatization of an act and we so called it in the voice-opening that was on the TV film, saying, "You're watching a dramatization of how real, how incredibly real, we think the picture is on Sylvania color television."

We have spent a great deal of time in our agency on the question of how do we get closer to persuasive advertising in view of the FTC's emotional state. We can't lie, we have to present documentation for every claim we make. The client, if anything—I'm talking about the responsible client and therefore I'm talking about the large and responsible agency—the client is perhaps more apprehensive about the ground rules today than the agency. Therefore, when you come over there with a piece of copy and/or a concept, he is not likely to say, well, for godsake that's no great claim, but what he will say is isn't there a sharper, more convincing way to state that claim which in itself we know is not so great and again it's back in our creative lap. Do we do it better than Mr. So-and-So down the street. Obviously, I'm prejudiced, I think we do.

Meadow was hardly alone in his warm appraisal of the agency he worked for. But DDB ran into some serious reversals in 1972, dropping about $30 million in billings. J. Walter Thompson, the world's largest advertising agency, lost about $50 million in billings in the last few years. Were both agencies on the skids, DDB's creative juice having run out and JWT's sales instinct and management skills having waned? *Advertising Age* editorialized the situation, suggesting that observers view the agencies' reversals from a historical perspective. Citing similar, earlier losses at Cunningham & Walsh and N. W. Ayer & Son, which had been recouped by those agencies, the marketing publication expressed confidence in DDB and JWT.

"The common thread in both . . . rejuvenated agencies," concluded the editorial, "seems to be that they both got back on the track of giving their people the responsibility and at the same time the freedom to come up with the big idea. We're confident JWT and DDB— momentarily off the track, it would seem—will do the same."

### THE COCKAMAMIE IMPULSE

Irrefutable and unfortunate as the fact is, before all the noise started in Washington, the advertising business was headed for a big fall, the kind of real thud that abuses invite. Frustrated by the hard realities of parity, shoved by clients who wanted a theme, a concept, a gimmick that would startle the cash register, and sometimes immobilized by its own sense of insecurity, Madison Avenue went overboard. It wasn't exactly a berserk situation, but truth was given the widest dimension so that many a lie was perpetrated in print and on the air.

The advertising practitioners even went a step further. The spurious claim hung on a fragile but compelling diversion—a cockamamie—became their metier and the order of the day.

The word is a corruption of decalcomania, the sticky, brightly drawn labels or signs transferred from one material to another and familiarly known as "decals." But cockamamies in the parlance of Madison Avenue assumed a totally different meaning. They became the new products, new ideas or "bold new" concepts that were intended to attract attention, bring in business and, through sparkling copy and fast-paced presentation, turn a consumer's concentration away from his actual and more vital needs.

Thus, airline advertising did—and still does—indulge in cockamamie approaches like movies in the clouds, stereo music that floods your ears, big comfortable lounges, attractive stewardesses turned waitresses, multicolored airplanes, dancing in the aisles, fashion shows, ad nauseam. All this when what the air traveler really wants is a safe trip in a plane that arrives and departs promptly.

Beer, cigarettes, soap, detergents and other commonly used products were given the cockamamie treatment starting at least a decade ago—and they have been getting it ever since. Now, maybe you're a beer drinker and easily offended when I tell you there is very little difference from one brand of brew to another. So any brand could have claimed it was "the one beer to have when you're having more than one" (implication, quality difference) or "if you've got the time, we've got the beer" (same implication).

Hampered by dicta from any longer being advertised on the air because of the cancer scare, cigarettes were superseded on the air waves by "little cigars," which really taste much more like cigarettes than cigars. These quickly were pushed in a manner to nauseate even those smokers who liked them. The best—or really the worst—example is the brand Winchester, happily labeled by its maker as "something else." This is not so bad in itself except that the accompanying action depicts the unbelievable behavior of a glum but hot-eyed westerner. Arriving on an airplane or helicopter, this thin-lipped loner barges in on an otherwise happy couple and by offering the girl a Winchester and a light whisks her away from her boy friend who, unhappily, is not thin, not a westerner, not a Winchester smoker. Is it really all that easy or are we having our leg (and our credibility) pulled?

But then, it's really not worse than some other cockamamies that are foisted on a tired and rapidly wearying public in many soap and detergent commercials— soap that immediately upon use propels you off the floor in an impressive demonstration of prestidigitation, detergent that descends on a community like a white tornado, bath soap that protects you all day long—from

© 153

what or is it *with* what? Cute, all cute, but why should anyone become a loyal customer? Ah, there's that parity again.

The gimmicks are so obvious, so clearly indicative of a lack of real difference in the product and a vacuum of creativeness on the part of both the marketers and advertisers that the public can hardly not be offended by the distaste, the exaggeration and, in many cases, the deception of these insulting appeals to a supposed low state of intelligence. The feeling of being offended is widespread and has been for a long time. But because it doesn't affect people—a mass slap-in-the-face or insult somehow doesn't have the sting that one delivered to an individual does—the unhappy reaction remains muted or simply festers under the surface.

"Cockamamies are a lot of things but most often they are apparent product or style changes," reports Martin Solow, former president and creative director of Solow/Wexton, a New York advertising agency. "In other words, you not only get a cockamamie but it wears out soon, too."

Is our economy based on cockamamies? A good question, not necessarily rhetorical, but the hapless consumer doesn't seem to care much, even today in the midst of a vociferous consumerism movement. Mostly he suffers in silence.

Harry F. Brian, president of VanSant Dugdale Advertising, Baltimore, looks on it all with some incredulity. "There is a lot of dumb advertising on the air," he says. "The people responsible for it must believe that the public is just plain dumb. You have to conclude it because advertising is always pegged to the audience level."

Adds Lester Lieber, chairman of Lieber Katz Partners, a New York City ad agency, "TV commercials are generally insulting to the intelligence of the more elite. Do advertisers set their commercials on the intelligence of the masses or what their own friends will go for? You develop your advertising along the lines you deem proper for the market but sometimes, and even more often, a client who depends on the agency for the creative spark will give you your head but when he sees what you come up with he complains, 'it's fine for you smart guys but we sell mostly to mid-America and we don't think it will go over there at all!' "

Among a few of the more cockamamie commercials cited by some of the more independent souls on Madison Avenue were:

"Alka-Seltzer-on-the-Rocks," a TV pitch obviously intended to transform use of the alkaline household remedy into an all-American drink. More or less discontinued after a while, the gimmick nonetheless prompted questioning as to whether it wasn't encouraging people to take "medicine" they might not need. The bottler of a competitive product, Brioschi, countered with his own campaign asserting that some alkalizers contain "drugs you don't need," like aspirin (Alka-Seltzer) or bromide (Bromo-Seltzer), while his doesn't.

And there is the typical Marge-and-Sally dialogue commercial, fortunately not used as much these days as it was just a few years ago. Two women in this particular perpetration stare starry-eyed at a room setting of new furniture. "Isn't this furniture beautiful?" asks one woman. "Yes, this is beautiful," replies the other. Enough said to convince the viewer at the other end of the tube? Yes, if they are sheep.

The third campaign of commercials was a laudable

one except that its execution, at least in the eyes of some critics, produced a reverse effect. It was the New York Urban Coalition's "Give-A-Damn" campaign in which typical examples of businessmen-black relationships or simply white-black relationships really represented virulent cases of racial prejudice. One of the most memorable sequences was a fat, cold-eyed white landlord showing some blacks a shabby apartment and saying, in effect, "Take it or leave it."

The "Give-A-Damn" campaign won a number of creative awards but what it did that it wasn't supposed to do was to dramatize the evil role of Whitey in the typical black ghetto. It had a backlash effect. It is frequently cited in Madison Avenue as an example of a creative concept that didn't have the salability it was meant to.

### THE FTC MEETS
### MADISON AVENUE

"We need the language of enthusiasm. We need the luxury of harmless puffery. We need the right to make those margins of superiority meaningful because they are the small steps on the stairway that lead to better products, greater satisfaction and more prosperity."

Incredible as such an admission may seem, these were remarks by Alfred J. Seaman, president of SSC&B, a prominent advertising agency, during the series of Washington hearings held by the Federal Trade Commission in the winter of 1971. Urging restraint in the drive for more and more facts or information in advertising, Seaman insisted that "poeticizing is different from deceiving." He also expressed some real concern about pressure for more and more "legalese" in the advertising profession.

But he was hardly done. The 160 interested and/or invited persons played the game during the sessions of carefully watching the faces of the five FTC commissioners in their high-back, black-cushion "thrones" as each witness spoke. There is, unfortunately, no record of any giveaway facial reaction by any commissioner to Seaman's next remarks.

Describing the "upward spiral" of improving products, he said, "breakthroughs are rare. It's like the high jump. Once you get over seven feet, the bar moves higher inch by inch, fraction by fraction. Products improve little by little, too. Competition soon catches the pioneer. The margins are small. Our job is to make those small margins of superiority meaningful to the consumer and then make the race for better products even swifter...."

He added, "Consumers don't consider every purchase so important as to make them want to study an encyclopedia. If you make us overload the ads with facts, you'll bore the consumer to death.... Advertising's usefulness will be greatly reduced. ... We are not only dealing with limited consumer fascination about product construction but we are dealing with very small advertising units. For example, about eighty percent of network television commercials are only thirty seconds long. By the time you establish your product and your proposition, there's not much time left...."

© 157

The five-week hearings were unprecedented. Not only was it the first time that the federal agency had taken such pains to earmark time, machinery and the opportunity to examine modern American advertising practices, but Madison Avenue was not the only one on the griddle. So was the FTC. Suddenly it appeared to have many critics charging that it was defaulting on its statutory right to protect the consumer by relying on cease-and-desist orders which proved to be enforcement taken long after the perpetrations charged had been ended.

During the first three days, when top advertising men had drawn glowing portraits of the benefits of advertising, the commission had listened impassively. But here and there some puffs of smoke erupted, signals that the commissioners had blood in their eyes. After Charles E. Overholser, research director of Young & Rubicam, described the research that is undertaken to prepare strategy on product advertising, Mary Gardiner Jones, an FTC commissioner, said, "There is no such thing as puffery because if you make a claim you intend to influence people."

"We don't expect metaphors to be believed," replied Overholser.

Referring to the extensive research, Commissioner Jones said, "If you don't expect people to believe it, then why do you use it?"

There were other flurries. Herbert E. Krugman, General Electric's manager of public opinion research, told the hearing that Starch studies show that only 9 percent of the readers of a publication read most of a particular ad. FTC commissioners expressed skepticism, however, particularly Miles Kirkpatrick, the agency's chairman. "An individual may not recall an ad," he observed, "but when exposed to the goods he may think favorably because of some subliminal association he acquired from the ads."

"The purpose of advertising is not to make ads popular," Krugman declared. "The advertiser is happy if people remember his brand and have a favorable impression."

Paul Rand Dixon, former FTC chairman who became a commissioner, said he was fed up with commercials repeatedly featuring testimonials by famous athletes, such as Tom Seaver and Gale Sayers. "Doesn't that affect recall? Isn't that why you pay these fellows all that money?" he asked.

There was little doubt that the witnesses paraded forth by the advertising community were persuasive, particularly those who didn't allow their self-righteousness to become too obvious. What was at issue—what advertising practitioners feared—was the possibility that Congress might allow the agency to increase its control powers through injunctive means to compel so-called deceptive advertising to be immediately discontinued. Thus a questionable campaign could be stopped before it could affect many consumers.

In that vein, C. W. Cook, chairman of General Foods Corporation, told the hearing, "We are not here to defend that which should be corrected. Neither are we here to do battle on behalf of the status quo when each of us knows that constant change is the law of life in a free economy. . . . We are here to affirm strongly that, while some regulation is needed and in the public interest, excessive restrictions on advertising will result in major damage to our economy and our society."

But the chairman of Pepsico., Inc., Donald M. Kendall,

took a hard-nosed view of the examination. "Much of the current discontent with advertising reflects a deepening misunderstanding or distrust of the whole American system of free enterprise," he declared. Kendall said he was able to trace some of the misunderstandings to "the almost total absence of basic economics courses in our public school systems. . . . And the distrust, I believe, is taught—often and all too well by men whose intentions for our country are either curious or unknown to me."

Advertising was often the whipping boy or the most convenient target for these people, Mr. Kendall said. "But, I think, the ultimate target is free enterprise itself."

Replying to the criticism that advertising persuades people to want the wrong things, he asserted, "I have little to say about this because it seems to me that either you accept freedom of choice as a basically democratic procedure or you don't. If we can't rely on individuals to make good product choices based on their own judgment, what may I ask is the next choice we will deny them?"

The debate waged on. . . .

Harold Demsetz, University of Chicago economics professor, said that the risk of serious misrepresentation in advertising was greatly exaggerated, mainly because advertising is exposed to millions of people and such exposure reduced the risk. "The free society keeps open the avenues of persuasion and it encourages us to walk along these avenues. What threatens the free society most is the blocking of avenues of persuasion."

Warren Braren, associate director, Consumers Union,

argued that what could be of "historic significance to the consumer" is the fact that during its hearings the FTC was looking at advertising from the inside out rather than the other way around. Heretofore, FTC has been given the end run on potentially deceptive advertising, possibly because of its failure to give due weight to the process and components employed in advertising. He added:

> The cigarette industry is currently responsible for a monumental sidestepping of both the commission and the Congress. Cigarette manufacturers, through vigorous promotion in the nonbroadcast media and the use of pictorial representations conveying a host of emotional responses, had been able to maintain the popularity of their products.
>
> Although cigarette companies were in some cases including health warnings and tar and nicotine content levels in their advertising, these disclosures are so camouflaged as to be rendered inconsequential in the total context of the ad. Even if the commission takes action to require a much more prominent disclosure of the warning, and of tar and nicotine levels, advertisers are capable of creating images which will largely bypass or negate the warning message.

Stephen A. Greyser, associate professor of business administration, Harvard Business School:

> While we know the public has a high tolerance of puffery in advertising, the atmosphere is one of increasing public skepticism in recent years as to whether advertising generally presents a true picture of the products advertised. ... At the same time we have seen growing skepticism, we have also consistently seen evidence that the public

© 161

thinks the standards of advertising are improving. The explanation is that the public is asking for higher and higher standards in commercial communications.

But if there was one area of possible overdeception that emerged from the hearings, it was on the advertising beamed at children. Among proposals made by witnesses were pleas to ban all TV commercials on children's programs and the establishment of a special FTC unit to develop and enforce a code for that type of advertising. A particular concern was expressed on the effect of child-oriented commercials on the eating habits of children. How would children react in future years to the heavy advertising they were now getting on such things as sugar-coated cereals, other types of sweets and candy-covered vitamins?

Witnesses pressed the point. That kind of food had nutritive shortcomings. Vitamin commercials not only encouraged hazardous self-medication by children but also tended to promote bad eating habits by suggesting, directly or implicitly, that vitamin pills were a worthwhile substitute for a good diet. One witness, Robert B. Choate, chairman of the nonprofit Council on Children, Media and Merchandising, cited a Saturday-morning commercial for Chocks, a vitamin supplement produced by Miles Laboratories. Fred Flintstone, the well-known TV cartoon character, "sells vitamin pills for kids to take 'when they don't eat right,'" Choate said.

Rather than considering children a special market with special needs, the television industry "considers children as just another market," declared Evelyn Sarson, who represented ACT (Action for Children's Television). "Not only does the industry find it acceptable to sell to children in this country," she added, "but the TV industry's own self-regulatory agency permits broadcasters to sell to children for sixteen minutes an hour—twice as long as they allow for adult prime time."

### AFTER THE HEARINGS, WHAT?

What was the upshot of the government's examination? Never before had the FTC been exposed to so much inside data from so many of the leading practitioners of the advertising business and never before had the great and frequently inaccessible Madison Avenue been exposed to such a revealing spotlight.

*Advertising Age* editorialized:

> Running through the hearing is that divergence of viewpoint which accounts for the continuing—and inevitable—difference between Washington and Madison Avenue. What is "persuasion" to Madison Avenue may be manipulation to Paul Rand Dixon, or "deception" to Mary Gardiner Jones. With the best of good will, the dividing point will always be unclear, so that it is foolish to expect that these questions will be finally resolved.
>
> What can be resolved, however, is a determination by both the industry and the commission to build on the relationships which have emerged from the hearing. There may not be any clear cut answers to many of these problems. But there is a mutual interest in continuing consultation which will help keep misunderstanding to a minimum.

© 163

What was also obvious to observers some months later in 1972 was that what the agency heard in its five weeks of hearings served to produce no worthy challenge to the more aggressive role the FTC had played in the two prior years in policing the advertising business. As a matter of fact, it was really the other way around. The mass of testimony had, if anything, strengthened the need to expand the regulatory function, especially in regard to children-oriented advertising. Within a matter of a few months, the new resolution on the part of the federal agency became dramatically clear.

At least three broadsides were hurled. The FTC called for companies using promotion that it considered deceptive to run corrective ads admitting their error. Then the commission proposed that broadcasters be compelled to give critics of commercials equal time to make counterclaims similiar to such things as antismoking ads. And then the agency let loose all its barrels, urging that the nation's four largest cereal makers be broken up into smaller companies, partially because their lavish advertising campaigns allowed them to foreclose competition and raise their prices. In addition, Kellogg, General Foods, General Mills and Quaker Oats were accused by Kirkpatrick's commissioners of falsely advertising their products as body builders and as aids to weight control.

But all this may be only the beginning. Already buffeted by the recession that began in 1970 which sharply cut profits and took a toll of about 10 percent of the jobs on Madison Avenue, the industry can only bleakly anticipate more restraints. The likelihood is that the hearings' findings will lead to tighter strictures on "puffery," the hard-selling hyperbole that is brought into play when advertisers have to face up to the realities of parity.

### BACK TO PETER PAN

Having come back, full circle, to parity, and the realization that more honest and yet more creative approaches are needed to inspire consumer interest in a particular product, it might appear that much ground has been gained. The advertising industry, in other words, had been battered into toeing the mark, jogged into a more responsible state resembling a form of maturity. It could now face the future, trembling but cleansed.

But such is not the case.

In June 1972, or about six months after the Washington hearings, the American Association of Advertising Agencies, the industry's biggest association, widely circulated a broadside by Professor Yale Brozen of the University of Chicago that the FTC's economic data was basically out of date and that the agency's notion that advertising raised the cost of products to consumers was an "old and obsolete" idea.

The basic economic doctrine on which the FTC was bringing complaints was already being discarded in economic analysis as erroneous and inconsistent with other parts of economic theory, Brozen said in a meeting of the AAAA's eastern annual conference. He explained that part of the problem was that the FTC did not recognize that advertising was a productive activity which

© 165

substitutes cheaply provided information for the expensive cost of each individual seeking information on products which he needs.

Earlier, Brozen, a professor of business economics at the University of Chicago's Graduate Business School and a business consultant, had received wide publicity as a voluble critic of FTC's actions against ITT Continental Baking Company. A consultant for ITT Continental Baking, Brozen had taken the position that the advertising of a product usually reduced the cost of the product to the consumer and that, if successful, the FTC's attacks on advertising will result in higher consumer prices.

Nevertheless, it was hard to swallow his contention that excessive claims and hyperbole were what Mrs. America needed in order to make her selections in the marketplace.

Now, Brozen—brazen Brozen?—also took the opportunity to challenge the agency's claim that the cost of advertising is a barrier to entry into markets. "On the contrary, advertising is a means to entry," he stated, "and should be viewed as the normal cost of going into a business just as building a store or plant would be viewed as an ordinary investment in entering a business."

His blasts and the AAAA's dissemination of them were only one of several clear indications that Madison Avenue was not through fighting the censure of its practices and that it was not at all in a mood of self-reproof.

The next straw in the wind was a revealing study undertaken by the American Management Association on truth-in-advertising. With research carried on mostly in the fall months of 1971 but followed up by interviews with industry, government and advertising practitioners, the study involved questionnaires sent to 1,275 marketing and advertising executives. It drew, in the AMA's own words, "an unusually low response of 150 usable replies."

Companies were fed up with the truth-in-advertising issue, the study found, with the requests for information being marked by "sophisticated buck-passing from one marketing executive to another . . . and by executives simply not responding to questionnaires, phone calls or direct letters addressed to them." Uniform standards are "desperately needed," for without them "advertising agencies experience great difficulty living up to their advertising commitments to both the company and the consumer and are often forced by economic priorities to choose the former."

Much attention, however, was being focused on the National Advertising Review Board, part of the Council of Better Business Bureaus, which will serve as a self-regulatory agency, monitoring the advertising practices of companies and agencies. And, the AMA survey found, 85 percent of the respondents felt that industry self-regulation would be "the most practical next step in solving the truth in advertising problem."

If a strong core of resistance existed on the issue before, during and even after the Washington hearings, others completely surrendered to the attack as if to indicate that their roles as advertisers or advertising practitioners had never been one of principle but of expediency. In my own researching on Madison Avenue, I was told by almost everyone I spoke to that "the creative days are gone, the careful, grim days are on us," or words to that effect. Put another way, in my own words, "If you can't stretch the truth, you can't be creative, because every product made and every service offered is no different than any other."

I submit that both premises are wrong. It is very possible to be creative without deceiving, and hardly all products and services are no different than any other.

Pressing these points to my interviewees, I was told that the problem was not with Madison Avenue but with its clients, the many big and small commercial and institutional clients who hire the agencies to sell their products or to achieve public identity for their services. The clients are the obstacles to truth—or the creative expressions of truth—because at first they wanted excitement and now they want safe dullness. The AMA study underscored the economic prod that exists between agency and client:

> Company power over an ad agency poses many problems. The topic of truth in advertising rarely comes up in company/agency meetings, so that guidelines are established only when the specific ad is reviewed.
>
> If an agency believes a company is more concerned with the bottom line total of a sales budget than with the degree of truth that accompanies the selling of a product, the agency may conclude that it has little choice but to create advertising that will meet the advertiser's goals. If an agency protests that the ad is not truthful, the company can easily find agencies that will advertise the product any way the company chooses. On the other hand, companies that desire a high degree of honesty, that have clear-cut and definitive objectives, that have communicated to their agency exactly what they expect will no doubt have

fewer problems, if any, with the FTC, consumers, and its sales objectives.

Does the client hold the reins of truth? Most agency heads think so. As Lester Lieber, head of Lieber Katz Partners, told me,

> If we are looking for some big changes, it will take the simple common sense of someone like the head of one of the major airlines to look honestly at his ads and say, "This is terrible—we've gotten too dull because we're afraid—I want something better!" I think agencies are capable of doing better, even in today's tough environment, than they have been but the difficulties of dealing with layers and layers of client management are a major obstacle. These are layers of timid people—they have the capacity to reject but not to accept. So the management holds the key if the structure will allow it to act decisively.

Like most other agency heads, Lieber is convinced that the burdens of intervention are greater on creative than on noncreative efforts and that this will stall changes for the better. "It's much easier to criticize innovative advertising as being deceptive," he said, "than it is to criticize it as dull."

If the practitioners are worried that the hot eye from the government and the consumerists will dry up the juices of creativity, it is also true that they have some very definite economy worries, too. Clients are not as sold on having agency tieups as they were before. More than 2,700 business leaders polled in a *Harvard Business Review* study in 1971 indicated that they thought too much was being spent on advertising, although most of them agreed that it was essential to marketing. But a growing number of advertisers, like General Foods, Pepsico, Pfizer and others are cutting costs of advertising by giving up the big agencies and dividing their work among small "boutique" agencies who specialize in various functions such as copy, artwork, market research and such. So the big agencies are finding that their full-service fees are eroding.

One can hardly ignore such trends at both the agency and the client levels. But one can argue with the use of the narrow lens with which advertising is generally viewing its problems. At a time when the public is obviously fed up with the pretension, deception, image-making manipulation in all walks of life, the commercial communicators appear to be blind and deaf to the demand for more low-keyed and simple messages, for honest creativity based on implicit qualities of product and service. Already, a "significant" 50 percent of ad men in the AMA sampling agree that sales would increase if advertising were more honest.

Not, it must be conceded, that it is an easy task to provide what the public evidently needs, for it is sometimes quickly spurned. After all, the nation's consumers have blithely ignored obvious efforts to improve their lives, such as the low-lead drive in gasoline to cut pollution, the cancer-scare campaign in cigarettes and the unit-pricing concept in food marketing which would redefine prices to all identifiable measurements.

Yet the challenge is clear. The nature of American society has changed radically, both fed and diverted by the populist and earthy tendencies of today's youth and by the vocal emergence of other social segments. If tell-it-like-it-is is an outmoded expression, then don't-tell-it-like-it-ain't might be more to the moment. Can the advertising business, its clients and its practitioners, throw off their Peter Pan syndrome, dip into their creative wells now covered by cobwebs and face up to their problems with some hardheaded honesty?

In order to relieve my frustrations, I decided on behalf of many other unhappy consumers to pen the following ode:

*To the Minions and Mavens of Madison Avenue*

Huff not, puff not.
Spare the cockamamies.
Scatter fewer gimmicks, put away the old tricks.
Trivia omnivia, hyperbole and adjectival stitchery resist.
Defensive puffery, audio- and video-borne, cease and desist.
Peter Pan, puerile one, hasn't your time passed?
Won't you grow up at last?

It appears quite reasonable that advertisers have not yet plumbed the truth of our times that emerges from one public attitude survey after another. A change in our values is running inexorably across the face and psyche of American society, scarred as it is after a decade of the most flagrant double-binding and deficit catering. And implicit in the new wishes of the consumer body is a yearning for simple talk, straight facts and the plain truth.

# 9.

## Public Relations—
## The Lindy's Waiters
## and the Super
## (PR) Men

IF MADISON AVENUE foists many a deception on the qualities of product and services, and if the public mistakenly and naively buys it, the practitioners of public relations are probably worse.

The New York public-relations community, the hub of the PR practitioner, is the most adept force in the world for manipulating images and perpetrating false identities. It's my firm opinion that many in that community could easily be hauled into the court of public opinion and charged with the high "crimes" of opinion engineering, value designing and truth stunting and for often acting against the public good in the interest of their clients. Mostly, it is the client—business, government, entertainment or institutional—who wishes to create the deception or, to put it more politely, to mold public opinion along specific lines that will help him. But it is the public-relations aide or consultant who carries it out in a manner that reflects his own contribution to the process. Is an accessory any less guilty than the actual perpetrator?

After more than a quarter-century as a writer and editor for two of the world's best-known newspapers, and before that for some of the country's most prominent trade papers, I have developed a hard-nosed attitude about the public-relations practice. And I have to admit that it is mostly negative. But, knowing that criticisms of what I wrote in this book would be acrid, that I would be charged with not taking a fresh look at how the practice has evolved, that I had only a one-sided viewpoint, I decided to have a series of interviews with a wide cross section of PR men. I also spoke to a number of clients of the PR community. Most of them expressed a negative reaction to the efforts of the communicators they used.

So why use them? Most of the businessmen I talked to shrugged, literally or figuratively. The more candid admitted that it was a matter of buying expertise to achieve the results they wanted. So what was the reason at its core? Greed? Insecurity? Competition? Yes, all of them. Honesty? Yes—and no. Does the average user of PR services feel that he cannot communicate his needs properly to the public? The shrug came on again among the interviewees, but the answer of those who would allow the discussion to go further was definitely—yes. The implication of this, of course, is that the public just doesn't know, can't understand and really doesn't care unless pushed into an understanding or a predesigned attitude.

Is it? Is the public a big don't-care, don't-know, don't-bother-me receptacle for all the attitude making that the publicity practitioner can successfully manage? After considering all that has happened in the last fifteen to twenty years to push the public into a variety of ideological corners, to accept political and social realities that are only fantasies when compared to what is really going on, to buy products that it doesn't want and services that it doesn't need and, above all, to act and behave wrongly because of all these false signals, it is hard to escape the conclusion that the public is as malleable as a handful of clay.

The situation is painfully simple. The public is unaware. And the principle is classic. The aggressor, reflecting the rules of warfare, is often successful. And so when played to his frustrations and fears (deficits), when subjected to opposing messages (double-binds) that are designed to create a mixed reaction such as "buy this" or "believe that" through fear, when handed deliberate falsehoods that corrupt the facts, the average American is as much a patsy for the hot-eyed, cold-hearted PR man as he is for the irresponsible advertising man.

I grant you that, like the advertising man who helps to move goods off the retail shelf and out of the industrial warehouse, the public-relations man moves information along the conduit from client to customer and from the institution to the public. It is a practical function.

But why does so much of that effort have to be slanted? Why does so much of it consist of lies? And why does the process have to be so patently a faucet that is turned on and off strictly for the client's benefit? Perhaps what we need are not only PR men but PRWs—public-relations watchers. Monitors of the publicity and communications channels who can blow a whistle when the lies begin to overwhelm.

### THE TENUOUS RELATIONSHIP

We are not so far from that stage now. A stage in which the vast bulk of Americans have lost confidence in many of our commercial, civic and social institutions because they no longer share the same goals. Yet, they must believe in them because they're the pillars that support our society; there is nothing else. So Americans are caught between a pervading disbelief and a wanting to believe in the values that have been created for them by the caretakers of those institutions.

Recently, I sat in the main dining room of Club 21, in Manhattan, surely one of America's premier restaurants, with a public-relations man whom I had known for some time. As I gazed around that lush dining room where the waiters were almost as thick as the customers, the prices unbelievable and the tables too close for comfort or confidences, I noticed a number of celebrities. Zero Mostel, the entertainer. Aristotle Onassis, the

© 175

Greek tycoon who had married Jacqueline Kennedy. Ethel Kennedy, widow of Robert F. Kennedy. Jack Valenti, the late President Lyndon Johnson's close aide and one-time president of the Motion Picture Producers Association. Also some quite well-known politicians and businessmen.

"I wonder why all these people come here," I said to my companion. "Any thoughts?"

The PR man, one I particularly liked because he could laugh at the child's game of public relations, replied, "They want to be seen here. It's the thing to do. Like everything else they do, it's the right framework for them. What do you want them to do—eat at Chock Full O'Nuts? They'd get no mileage out of that."

"So why do they keep looking around the room?"

He laughed and shrugged. "Comedian. Why shouldn't they? Is there a law against it? They're watching each other. They're always watching each other. That's the game they play. If somebody gets one up on them, they got troubles. So they're keeping tabs on everybody."

"So why did Toots Shor go out of business up the street?"

"You tell me."

Later, as I recalled this sparkling interchange while contemplating the low state of public belief and confidence in government, business, the military and many of our social bodies, it struck me that maybe it came from the fact that too many leaders were spending too much time studying each other, worrying about their competitive positions, concerned that someone else "gets one up on them," rather than concentrating on serving the public. So the service rendered was superficial, a cosmetic effort rather than a substantive one.

And what it was creating was a withering of public credibility. In everything, it seemed.

Government confidence had certainly declined. Republican or Democrat in its stewardship, it didn't seem to matter. Even overwhelming mandates didn't seem to change it since alternatives were few. The principle of the double-bind is exploited nowhere as much as in politics and public life while the play to, and the capitalization on, the average person's inner deficits are common.

Business, too, is probably in its lowest state of credibility in decades. The bribe, the kickback, the quid pro quo concept of favor-for-favor, the patronage, the executive embezzlements, the smell of an unsavory relationship between some business elements and government—all have served to support long-time private skepticism over businessmen's goals. But the PR man tries to smooth over the growing cynicism, sometimes successfully and more often not. As one said to me not long ago about the irresponsibilities of his client, "What can I do with the s.o.b., change his glands?"

Our financial institutions are in trouble because of the lack of confidence in which they are held by the public. Wall Street, with gyrations and movements that often seem to have no connection with economic forces, has proved to be a trap in recent years for many small investors who have seen their stockholdings dwindle in value. Who sets the pace; who calls the shots; who moves Wall Street? Not many of the 35 million investors but the big buyers and sellers, such as institutional portfolio holders, banks, insurance companies, mutual funds. The great tides they precipitate in trading and in stock values frequently leave the little investor with declined equity and little understanding of what has happened, except the vague feeling that he has been taken.

Over the last few years, inside knowledge that often allows its holders to capitalize on it has increasingly marked stock trading. It is my guess, largely unsupported, that the infrequent cases of illegal insider stock trading that surface in a charge or citation by the Securities and Exchange Commission are only a fraction of what really goes on. I'm hardly alone in that conviction. Most people even faintly familiar with stock market and business practices would hardly disagree.

What is the value of the public-relations man in business? If he is in product publicity or marketing public relations, he works to help his client sell goods by pushing its qualities and needs in a companion effort with advertising. If he is a financial PR type, his role is entirely to raise the value of his client's stock, regardless of how he may couch his activities such as "building corporate image" or "bringing us closer to the security analyst."

But corporate behavior defies what even the wiliest PR man can cover up. Frauds in housing loans, paid-for recommendations of a clean bill in financial transactions, ignoring the stockholder in many key corporate decisions that seriously affect his holdings, the ever-continuing floating of new equity issues creating layer on layer of Chinese money are a few of the other behavior characteristics of many companies. The wonder of it all is the acceptance of such acts by the public, or at least the lethargy that the average American investor or even noninvestor demonstrates in the face of such antics.

Is the businessman the unwilling villain? Is he caught in a vise of being compelled to perform at virtually any cost or with any means and the burdens of competition, taxes, government controls and public and private censure? And what of the role of the public-relations adviser or staff man? Is he an unwilling accessory? Too many PR men I know complain, as do advertising men, that many clients don't listen to advice but go their own way after toting up the risks and warnings of their PR aides. How many outside public-relations advisers get up when they see that they are being ignored and give up the account on principle? Not many, not many at all.

Who holds the responsibility for truth, integrity, and accuracy in the client-adviser relationship? Do PR people get the same respect as other advisers? Why is business losing credibility? These were some of the questions I asked as I got around the public-relations business and here are some of the answers:

Richard W. Darrow, chairman of Hill & Knowlton, the biggest PR firm in the United States and abroad, said, "The real problem is that some management people have never fully accepted the advice that they get from public relations. They fail to equate it with the advice they get from their legal and accounting advisers. In general, top management acts on a smaller percentage of the advice it gets than it should and as a result sometimes fails to avoid a catastrophe."

As an example, Darrow cited one big company (unidentified) that invests more money in environment protection activity than any other. Its outside public-relations advisers caution it to be careful to keep its own house clean while engaging in widespread antipollu-

© 179

tion acts. But somewhere along the line, one company plant dumps phosphate into a nearby lake or ammonia into a local river. The resultant outcry, says Darrow, quickly submerges all the other antipollution efforts the concern has been taking.

"Perhaps what's needed nowadays," suggests Darrow, who has been both staff and outside PR man for years, "is an understanding something like the old-time town-hall meeting where you get up and admit what you've done and try not to fool anyone. That's how credibility comes. Management today spends a lot more time worrying about social consequences than twenty years ago and still it has an inadequate realization that one rotten apple makes the whole barrel smell."

But business is under severe bottom-line pressure— so who will do anything in the public interest that will hurt that bottom line? There's a delicate balance between keeping the corporate incentives and bearing up under proliferating government controls. "So the question becomes—how much credibility do you deserve?" But the ballgame is changing because of heightened corporate social awareness. "The environmental pressures are causing business to listen more to the PR man, and management is listening better now." Too many people already have a vested interest in watching whether business has a sincere social awareness for businessmen to ignore it.

George Hammond, chairman of Carl Byoir & Associates, the second largest PR firm in the world, is convinced that one of the curses of the public-relations field is the delegation of authority in corporate life which insulates the PR function from top management. "But this is one of the functions that can't be kept from top management because the issues involved can be deep and pervasive," Hammond said. "In the intensity of a problem that suddenly heats up, the ball will suddenly be thrown to the chief executive by Congress, the press, even the Courts."

According to Hammond's top associate, Robert J. Wood, Byoir's president, image making is becoming less personal and more institutional. Perhaps this came about because the more recent breed of chief executive is less of a showman, less of an individualist and much more of a team man and thus inclined to keep a low profile. Did this mean that the businessman, reflecting the more pallid but perhaps more premeditated CEO, was retreating behind a façade of impersonality?

Hammond didn't think so. "Who knows the names of the ten biggest companies nowadays?" he countered. "The strong personalities have given way to professional managers, administrators who believe that corporations get their reputations from performance, not from individualistic owners. And what they also realize is that a popular company in the eyes of the community is the one which creates the aura of standing for something or doing something or of having accomplished something that gets its name favorably mentioned around. This is a major way in which many companies have attempted to show their social conscience—the integration with the needs of the community."

"Getting a handle on the company," as Wall Street analysts often describe it, is one of the toughest things for management to achieve in terms of image, said Frank Malley, president of Doremus & Co., a major financial public-relations and advertising agency.

"The point is—a company chief has to have the ability

© 181

to analyze what his business is so as to make it compre-
hensible to outsiders or any audience that he deems
important. To the extent that a client will let a PR agency
help—and not all do—this can usually be accomplished," Malley said. But, he added, the challenge was,
as one company president put it, "We've got six thousand salesmen out around the country selling our products. But who is selling our company and what are we
trying to sell anyway?"

However, James Cope, president of Selvage, Lee and
Howard, didn't quite see it that way. In fact, he got a
little incensed about it.

"I've always been allergic to the idea that a company
has to be loved," he said. "Who the hell wants to go to
bed with a company? It's a little like the attitude toward
a military leader. He may be a louse but if he wins
battles and saves the lives of his own troops because of
aggressive methods, the troops will go through hell for
a good officer. It should be the same for a company."

So the solution, in Cope's view, is for managements to
stress what their businesses are doing directly and indirectly to improve education, raise employment, help
the metabolism of a city by controlling pollution. And
all of it is easily attainable, he said, once businessmen
get to understand the need.

"Public relations will have to upgrade itself and be
run by better and better people. The giving in of business to avid consumerists, regardless of the merits of the
issues involved, has been nothing less than a vote of no
confidence in the PR man. Business got scared—but it
shouldn't have been. . . . It already had a lot going for it
in terms of what it was doing for society, only it wasn't
adequately telling its story." So said Cope.

### THE RATTLED CLIENT

On all fronts, a strain of fear or at least serious concern runs through the upper tiers of business, government, academia, culture and entertainment.

Whether it is a chairman of the board getting the shakes over ecology, consumerism or the spinning values of his stock, or a top government official worried about his tenuous constituency or the militancy of minority or feminists' groups or a university chancellor fearful of a resumption of campus sit-ins and demonstrations, somehow they always turn to public relations to solve their problems. The odd thing about such a move is that it usually denotes a superficial solution is in the works. Not always, perhaps, but usually.

Calling in the PR expert first literally shows that the "client" considers the problem one that has arisen from outside causes. A congressman who craves greater acceptance among the blacks calls in a black or probably a black-oriented PR man. A conglomerator who is still worried about his price-earnings multiple brings in a PR man who has a reputation for building up P/E. An entertainer anxious to bolster a fading name puts a PR man to work on it. In each case, the assignment is to change the individual's image, the exterior aspect. Rarely is it to attack the root problem, the faults that exist within the client's makeup or his organization that are basically responsible for the unhappy image.

Sometimes the PR adviser tries, suggesting and even

urging the client to change his policies to improve those traits that are most closely reflected in the client's image. But it's a tough road, because if that is what the client wanted, who needs the PR man? Instead, an efficiency expert, a management consultant, would have been hired. And the client might not even have listened to him.

But because the fears and concerns of those who sit under the harsh, white spotlight have risen in recent years, the public-relations man has been transformed from a simple image maker to a merchant of new identities in financial, social, ecological, urban and consumerism areas. Environment-ecology, consumerism and financial relations were the subject of background materials most often asked for in 1971 by the members of the Public Relations Society of America. In the interviews I had with Richard Darrow and William A. Durbin, chairman and vice-chairman of Hill & Knowlton, I asked them which six subjects most concerned their clients these days. Their answers, not necessarily in order of priority, were:

1. The energy gap in oil, gas, utilities
2. Foreign competition
3. Multinational problems—the double-edged sword of tightening domestic competition pushing corporations to venture abroad and the crackdown by foreign governments and corporations on invaders from the United States
4. Environmental and consumerism issues
5. Labor costs, a rising curve that aggravates the problem of foreign competition
6. Disclosure problems of all kinds, intensified since the

federal and state governments and the securities exchanges stiffened the disclosure rules

Rightly or wrongly, the grasping for solutions by hiring public-relations men for the staff or as advisers has opened many new opportunities for those people. Robert J. Wood, president of Carl Byoir, noted that the PR business was poised for a major upsurge. After three relatively flat years, 1969 through 1971, with 1972 having picked up in tempo, the new wave of dominant issues was making the public-relations man once again a significant figure on the corporate scene. The PR man is a sort of doctor, he implied, with some evident seriousness.

In earlier years, he said, major issues propelled public relations to an important role. These included the Great Depression's antibusiness mood; the strictures on Wall Street enforced about the same time by the Securities and Exchange Commission; the rising labor movement in the thirties and forties; the emergence of militant blacks, young radicals and feminists in the fifties and sixties; and the time of the raider and the conglomerates in the sixties and early seventies. Each proved a bonanza for the public-relations man.

Now, a new bonanza wrapped around touchy, developing issues appears to be beckoning for the PR practitioner. But the question is, How much of his renewed use will represent only a superficial effort? Past experience leads any dispassionate observer to doubt that it will be anything more. As was so often the case in the past, client and publicity man will try to convince everyone that the performance deserves the applause of all.

After all, if they say it long enough and loud enough, if the message has all the outward essentials of plausibility, who is astute enough to resist it all? Who, indeed, except those who are astute—and do resist—and are growing in numbers.

Let's consider why so many corporate, government and other leaders are really concerned. For one thing, public images are based on many things; while failure in one or more may hurt, it is the combination of factors that creates the total exterior aspect.

But the objective of having a fine, the best, competitive image has an ulterior motive rather than being an end to itself, a justified recognition for intrinsic performance. For businessmen, it means being able to get to the head of the line at the bank in an era of tight money or of seeing their stocks rise in value. For politicians, it means reelection and basking in the broad mandate that signifies strong support for acting or not acting on pending legislation. For academicians, it means attracting the financial patronage and maintaining the respect that provides the viability of a university. For those in the worlds of culture and entertainment, image is all since it relates directly to support, position and survival.

Yet how much does the client exert himself to improve his institution of whatever its nature when he acts on his concern by hiring the communicator? Is the simple truism of earning one's reputation losing its meaning? Or, to put it politely, is image everything but everything?

## THE LINDY'S WAITERS AND
## THE SUPER (PR) MEN

Everyone knew of him, everyone in the metropolitan New York, Chicago and Los Angeles and other regional media, printed and airborne. The biggest braggart, the sliest angle man, the flashiest publicity counselor, all deceptively wrapped up in a low-key delivery, a Brooks Brothers pin-stripe suit with button-down-collar shirt and rep tie. For years he had built himself up as the press expert except that he wasn't close to more than a handful in the press who were, like him, self-aggrandizers and some of them not reluctant to have their itchy palms painted green.

"You want the moon, the stars—hell, you want the cover of *Time?*—I can get them for you. Just leave it in my good hands," he would pitch prospective clients. Pressed for details, he had them, such fine points as:

"It's not the truth that pays off—it's the front you put on that delivers."

"Let's not bother with those $10,000 to $15,000-a-year newspaper hacks. You want to push the price of your stock up? We'll do better with one of those $50,000 security analysts."

"Don't confuse me with all the facts. Let's see how far I can go with just a few of them."

He is and was a fantastic individual. Before he cooled down a bit (he had some personal problems), he was hired by many clients and exploited most of them. Using the promises he was famous for and the razzle-dazzle approaches that angered other PR people, not to mention the press, he stole a $100,000-a-year account from under the nose of a much larger public-relations agency. Although it is part of the industry's code of ethics that no public-relations firm should solicit a client who already has an agency, he did it anyway.

For identification purposes, let me call this fellow Bob Johnson, although that is not his real name. Now he is not a typical PR agency owner, at least not completely. But it is my experience that at least some dimension of our moon-stars-*Time* friend exists in virtually all PR men, breathes deep within them and comes to the surface often. That is, among the PR men I know—and I know a lot of them.

In fact, to use the cliché that has come to be the mark of the hypocrite (I hope of course that I am not), "Some of my best friends are PR men." This is not untypical of many newspapermen. But as I observe the actions of many public-relations people and listen to their problems, I have come to realize that they are mostly men and women caught in a trap into which they have willingly stepped or lowered themselves. The trap is a simple one of a classic type. By hiring themselves out to help their employer to establish or improve his identity to his customers, constituency or contemporaries, they have agreed to accept his own assurance that he merits such an identity. The communications professional, as his part of this troubled pact, has in effect promised to provide his client with an effective program that is legal and ethical. But success is its payoff criterion. Thus the moon-stars-*Time* promise lurks in every client–PR relationship. Each is a relationship that depends on mutual reliance and responsibility. And such are the frailties of human nature, among which are imbedded deep veins of chicanery and greed, it is a relationship fraught with risk and even danger. But for whom?

Client, PR practitioner and public—which gains and which loses in such relationships? Let's try some recent situations and see.

In the late 1960s, the president of a publicly owned manufacturing concern was sorely troubled because he had been cited by the SEC and faced litigation for alleged stock manipulations. The agency claimed that he had deliberately made misleading statements in order to force up the price of his stock. And when the SEC issued its citation and then filed a court suit against him, he was rocked to his core. He told everyone that he felt shamed before his family and associates.

Calling in a financial public-relations agency, he instructed it to place stories on how good his company was and how it had contributed in many ways to the community. He couldn't be quoted in any direct way on the financial performance of his company because it was "in registration." A stock issue which he had proposed was still to be approved by the SEC and the agency's rules precluded him from appearing to influence potential investors in his pending new issue. "What I want is to secure my company's reputation at this time because of the litigation," he told the PR adviser. "You see, it's this way—I don't want my family to be pointed at and I want my employees to be as proud to work for me as they have always been."

So the efforts got under way. Of course, it wasn't easy. First, the press was skeptical. Second, the client didn't like what finally appeared in the media because each writer felt impelled to mention the litigation as part of the company's status. Third, he kept confusing the public-relations agency because he insisted, "Don't give me any personal publicity," even though the company was an elongated reflection of his own drives and quirks. And this emerged clearly in all interviews and was duly reported.

The results of this stew of confusion and misdirection helped no one—the investing public, the millionaire's family and his employees least of all. The PR agency, after a period of frustration and ineffectiveness, threw up its hands and quit. Then, and only then, did it learn the truth. The manufacturer's trauma over the court suit was only a superficial expression of his real trouble. That lay in his home life, involving difficulties with his much younger wife with whom he had been incompatible for some time. Seeking some sort of a simplistic solution to his real problem, he had hoped to find it in recognition by the press. Only it didn't come.

Another businessman eager to solve his problems in the press wanted just the reverse. He craved personal publicity and hounded his agency for it.

"He was an egomaniac," his PR man told me. "He didn't need publicity about himself because he was already well known. What he really needed was a better image for his company. The times were bad for his particular kind of business and besides he had gotten himself into trouble on so-called racial discrimination in his employment practices."

But, the "egomaniac" would often turn off the positive public relations aimed at correcting his corporate problems in favor of seeking his name in the paper.

"It was just pure ego satisfaction—if it wasn't on him, his charities, his horse-racing activities and so forth— what he kept constantly pushing for was space on his family and his beloved daughter," his PR man recalled. "One thing he was crazy about was to be considered a great sportsman and that was one of the main things he insisted we push. The company, which really needed a break, could just go to hell."

This situation began to reach a ridiculous state. In the mid-sixties, there was a generally meaningful connection or duplication of readers among the *New York Times, New York Herald Tribune* and the *New York World-Telegram & Sun* who might well be considered a market for this individual's business. But there were some of the same market for him among the readers of the *New York Daily News* and the *New York Journal-American.* Yet the businessman at first insisted on being the subject of a *New Yorker* magazine article and then announced that he would accept as a substitute a personal feature in the *Times.* All the other media didn't have it as far as he was concerned. And eventually he got his *Times* story.

The peak of his zany push for personal publicity was reached when he decided to run a special $50,000 *New York Times* Sunday supplement. "He put the arm on all his suppliers to advertise and that was how it was financed," said his PR adviser. "And of course there were four separate pictures of him scattered through the supplement, and the lead article had to be on his family and its history. There was even a page on his sporting activities. The whole thing was a twenty-four-page retelling of the Horatio Alger story."

Who won in that entire, sad public-relations caper?

No one, certainly not the businessman and his company.

Well remembered in publicity circles is another client, a dynamic real-estate developer, who literally pushed himself to death. An ambitious, overzealous type who often worked around the clock, sometimes going seventy-two hours at a stretch with only two hours of sleep in between, this man lived days and nights on end on peanut-butter sandwiches and milkshakes. But so attuned was he to creating publicity himself that he really didn't need any help from professional PR men.

Still, he hired one. The PR man's main job was to keep his client awake. He did it, too, until one day the client, sadly enough, dropped dead.

Eventually every client becomes a Lindy's waiter.

This is a conviction among many public-relations men, a conviction arrived at after long experience. Lindy's waiters, you may or may not know, were long considered the prima donnas, the peacocks, the ballerinas of the Broadway dining circuit. If, for example, you were to complain to a Lindy's waiter as he brought you a bowl of soup that he had put his thumb into it, he would probably reply with a snarl, "Don't worry about it, Charley. The chef don't mind!" That, of course, is a variation of that old chestnut about the waiter's reply when the customer tells him there is a fly in the soup: "Don't let it upset you. We won't charge extra!"

Clients of the PR community, too, become so sold on their own wisdom, knowledge and skills that they tend to tell their PR advisers how to conduct themselves in their own field. And the Lindy's waiter complex thrives on itself.

But if the client thinks he is a superman, my own experience has found, he is only a puny one compared to most PR men. Many are convinced that they hold the press in their hands and that they are the puppet masters to the journalist's puppet. Over the years, I've developed a feeling of exasperation on the antics, the egomania and the shenanigans of many I have run into.

PR men I have known:

*King Cole, the Merry Old Cad.* Jovial, three-chins' chunky, a veritable old-timer who has been around for a long time and doesn't let you forget it. King Cole was a buddy to many newspapermen and women, forever remembering their birthdays and anniversaries. But when one of them needed to get through to one of his clients on a touchy matter, he was always in transit or on the phone or somehow just not available to assist in making the contact. Yet, when the client had a favorable release, or wished to meet the press to make some unimportant announcement, King Cole was all efficiency, dispatch and even managed to be on hand to host the press conference. I guess what really annoyed me most about this phony was his claim that he was on wonderful terms with the press. He wasn't with me.

*Glib-Glub, the Empty Head.* A common type is the brisk, youngish agency "senior vice president" or vice president, an efficient, knowledgeable guy who could write well, speak glibly but never seemed to have an angle on a story. "Meet my client—you'll enjoy him— and he's heard a lot about you," was the usual request. Should a story result as it did more than once, the PR man would dash off a gracious letter of thanks. But the client never took the trouble to do so. A minor oversight, probably. But then it occurred to me that this was probably because the client had been convinced by the hot-shot that it was all his doing, even down to the very angle that he had never suggested. But it really didn't matter. My publisher pays my salary, thank heaven, not the client. But I don't deal with that hotshot anymore. I never did need him. Yet, as a chronicler of the mores of people in business among other activities, I would have loved to hear the claims that the PR man made to the man who paid his fees. Some of the best conversations, I'm afraid, are those you never hear.

*Honest Benny, He'd Never Steal a* ——. This one really gets under my skin, not unpleasantly, but because his earnest honesty and kindness made me feel uncomfortably obligated to him. He was so determined never to be accused of favoring his clients that all his suggestions for stories were negatively flavored. "You wouldn't want to meet the president of ——? No, he's so full of crap that I wouldn't want to wish him on you." Or, "Look, this guy is coming to town and he'd like to talk about his new diversification program. Personally, it sounds like a lot of zip to me but—" At such meetings, he would fight for you and even argue in a nice but determined way with his client to get you the facts that you pressed for. But I couldn't take him either. He was just too much. He would give me that tight feeling around the temples. Don't help me so much, dammit! I wanted to yell at him. But how can you yell at such a nice guy?

*The Personal, Perpetual Pleader.* "I know it doesn't mean much to you, just another story, but it would mean a hell of a lot to me." This was the way this PR man, a six-foot-six, massive, former collegiate-football star would pitch me. His size totally belied his snivelling manner. Underneath his tough, bulldog face, a pool of steaming uncertainty bubbles. But he and others like him somehow rarely take no for an answer. Even telling him the truth didn't matter. That editors have the final say on stories, not reporters; that putting things in a personal way was all wrong and unfair; that if a reporter allowed personal pleas to be a criterion, it would eventually and completely kill his usefulness. None of it registered, even when I spelled it out. But this guy turned out to be resourceful anyway. After he failed to attract my interest, I learned that he told his clients that the reason I didn't do the story was that I probably had something "personal" against him.

*The Only Lovely PR Men—the Ladies.* I'm being kind, of course, because although I work at being difficult, I'm not as much of a pain in the neck as some others I've worked with. But I've dealt with plenty of the lady PR types and not all are lovely, although they are generally as efficient as their male counterparts, whatever that means. But I must report, too, that many of the ladies tend to use the personal plea, like "it would really mean so much to me," and I have found it doubly annoying. In a few rare cases, the pleas even turned to promises and twice to propositions. But I'm prompted to say that I held fast. The good PR ladies, though, almost but not quite make up for the highly emotional ones.

*That Butterfly, Harry.* This PR man has his fingers, nose and feet into everything, so many different situations that it's hard to take him seriously. Wherever you go, he's there, tapping you on the shoulder and hurriedly introducing you to someone whose name always sounds like "Chasfrast" or "Ungerdown." Should you be foolish enough to get involved with him and one of his clients, the frustrations are endless. There's rarely a real story there, and Harry flits around never quite knowing where you can pin down his client or just what the facts are that you need. But when you get him on the phone, he says that since he's got you there's another client, too, and if he could just interest you in—. Incidentally, this man has an interesting technique that he also uses to add to the confusion that he creates otherwise. Since he likes to keep everyone who works for him on their toes, he takes pains never to let them know when he's in or out. He slips out through a secret back door to his office after locking his office door from the inside. His secretary works in an outer office so even she never knows whether he is there or not. So there is no point even trying to call him. He's probably out buttering Chasfrast or Ungerdown.

So there they are. Six PR men I've known and I probably could go on for a while filling out the list. But I feel I've made my point. I'm just not very happy with most of the PR men I know. They may be super to their clients who may also be super to them. But as far as I am concerned, I wish they wouldn't patronize me, fool me, implicate me, take advantage of my feelings, proposition me or frustrate me—and I haven't even mentioned those, admittedly few, who have tried to bribe me.

Like the advertising man, the public-relations executive or counselor has his meaningful function—providing the link between the decision makers and the media. And I'm not really as irascible, as unreasonable, as difficult or as much the PR-man's dragon as I may seem. Between 1962 and 1972 on the two major newspapers which employed me, my conservative estimate is that I wrote at least two thousand stories, working with many public-relations people in the process. So my relationship with the PR community must have been at least reasonably fruitful.

But one thing really bothers me. Why can't they settle just for the whole world instead of the moon and the stars?

# 10.

## The Press—
## The New Game Is
## to Kick It Around

UNDER SIEGE

THE WAY THINGS are going, if they keep going that way, Americans may not in the future have the media to kick around anymore. At least, not in the free form that they were created by the Founding Fathers and in the manner that they were protected by the First Amendment, which after all preceded all the rest of them.

Perhaps the biggest put-on of all, the biggest double-bind, the most flagrant feeding to our deficits, has been the discrediting of the press and the media in general from both ends of the political spectrum, the government, the activists and militants, the consumer advocates and almost everyone else. The worrisome thing is that in the sad story of moribund civilizations one of the most indicative signs was the muzzling and enforced deterioration of the public channels of communications.

Yet, if the leaders of our society and their professional communicators bend honesty, err on their own behalf and fool the public most of the time, much is wrong, too, with the media which is basically their vehicle of expression as well as the public's.

Some faults are obvious. In the newspapers it is speed which surrenders accuracy, oversimplification, overdramatization, lack of follow-up, negativism, use of uninformed reporters, slanted circulation efforts, to mention only a few. In magazines it is pandering to readers in terms of mass-circulation impact, sensationalizing, superficiality and indulgence of specialized prejudices. In television and radio it is one-sided reporting, encroachment of advertising into editorial performance, uninformed journalistic execution, a stress on violence and negativism.

There is no doubt that many of the printed media's faults are intrinsic in their systems. If editorial-advertising ratios call for a rigid breakdown in the interest of economics, editorial matter is often sacrificed. If a major story breaks at or near deadline, its coverage will not be as full, as balanced or as skillful as if the story had broken hours earlier. And, as the size, pace and intricacy of the media have grown, their faults have grown, too.

Critics have charged, with at least some justification, that proprietors of the media are responsible for many faults of their services because they are mostly interested in profits. The bottom line remains the criterion supreme on the viability of the newspaper, magazine and radio-TV station. This priority will scarcely wane under the increasing concentration that marks media ownership, which in the case of many newspapers reaches to monopoly level. Why should media management ripple the waters, possibly affecting advertising revenue, when profits might be hurt? The better media owners have the answer: a better product.

Nevertheless, under the lash of criticism from all sides and the risk of profit erosion from pursuing a forthright, even courageous stance, the behavior of media owners in the next few years raises a big, not so hypothetical question: To protect their flanks and cash registers, will the media proprietors capitulate sufficiently to stay alive and preferably to thrive? Or, will it become another matter of material success breeding a failure in obligation?

With 75 percent of all commercial television stations owned by chain management and the number of daily newspapers having dropped from about 2,500 in 1910 to about 1,750 in 1972, the hardy independent medium which could go its own individualistic way certainly appears to be headed for extinction. Will those caught in the spreading concentration have the desire and the incentive to sustain the enterprising efforts that characterized the earlier forms of the media? Not very likely, the recent record shows.

### THE BESIEGERS

In many ways, the federal government has taken over the principal newsmaking role in America, squeezing the media in general or favoring those that have been willing accessories. Individually, the Washington administration's acts to control what is and what isn't news do not appear to be disturbing. But when seen collectively, the aspect can be alarming.

Are the political and ideological considerations to be allowed to be the sieve through which news will be filtered? It's hard not to build up a strong conviction that we are witnessing just that:

Washington can and has assumed control of national television and radio in prime time at will. Some of this has had definite political overtones.

The Presidency, both by prestige and by order, can virtually preempt the news with visits to Berlin, Moscow and Peking.

What are classified or unclassified documents? On classification of strategic materials or their declassification, the federal bureaucracy makes its own rules and sets its own timing. How much is the public entitled to know? Many disclosures not pertinent to national security are withheld for reasons that are more personal or political than anything else.

Like a petulant corporation chief or nervous football coach, the government plays games of hot-and-cold with the media. It gives news on a selective basis to friendly journalists or media. As in the November 1972 incident in which President Nixon bestowed a detailed interview on the *Washington Star and News* in order to put down the *Washington Post* which has been particularly critical, the administration isn't reluctant to use its principal office to slap some journalistic wrists.

It can and does penalize uncooperative reporters by withholding accreditation or by leaking tips to their direct competitors.

Misinformation (as in the case of the U-2 flight over Russia), blackout (as in the Bay of Pigs and Laos invasions), the backgrounder interview (as many times given by recent Presidents) are all attempts to channel the news by withholding all or a large part of such major developments.

Vice-President Spiro Agnew excluded the newspapers from a speech he gave to the television networks, a speech that was exclusive but which ironically involved severe criticism of the networks.

On the other hand, Chief Justice Warren Burger banned the air media from some of his speeches because he admittedly didn't like their "selection" of excerpts.

Sometimes the pressures are economic, but they indirectly affect the media's news-reporting ability. Under the new "fairness doctrine," the Federal Communications Commission can compel television broadcasters to give important time to those who feel they have been penalized by commercials. This could prevent advertisers from continuing to advertise, denigrate their creativity, hurt network business, engage the listeners' attention to a meaningless debate and eventually affect the stations' news-reporting activities through a decline in revenues. TV broadcasters are already losing money on news reporting.

The FCC also exerts a censoring function through its renewal licensing. Pressures have been generated to bring broadcast media in line on a nonrenewal threat.

Federal and local courts have subpoenaed reporters for both print and broadcast media to reveal their sources of information and surrender their records. (Even business reporters can become involved this way. Some years ago, I was subpoenaed as a witness for the complainant in a trademark infringement case being heard in a federal district court. When I was asked for the notes that I was also ordered to bring along, I replied that they were "company records" as I had been instructed to by the company's counsel. I was lucky. I was curtly dismissed.) An increasing number of newsmen have been jailed.

The trend to exclude reporters from courtrooms is in itself an alarming one. How will the public know if justice in the courts is being maintained unless it reads on-the-spot reports or participates in the jury function? Perhaps it is small wonder that the credibility of the courts has withered when the judges contribute to suspicions by barring the press.

And what of probes by the Federal Bureau of Investigation of some prominent newsmen, such as Jack Anderson, the columnist; Neil Sheehan of the *New York Times;* and Daniel Schorr of Columbia Broadcasting System? I grant you that reporters may go off the deep end in one way or another—like everyone else—but I have yet to run across more than a grouser, let alone a subversive, in more than twenty-five years of working side by side with many. But investigations of the press by the FBI have an awesome ring with frightening overtones.

The federal government, its agencies, the courts and the FBI are hardly the only ones which by their actions are both limiting and discrediting the press.

Business contributes to the siege by default, showing a pervading fright when it must disclose negative news and failing to respond with confidence if not courage when it is assailed by government or activists.

The Gay Liberation, the feminists, the Black Panthers and many specialized lobbying groups in labor, agriculture, and extremist politics have accused the press of biased, lazy, superficial reporting. And what is ironical is the fact that many media have duly reported all of it. Spiro Agnew certainly could not complain of the space and prominence his criticisms of the media have been given in the same media that he blasted. But there is little doubt that the broadsides by the vice-president and others have seriously hurt the press's public image.

Two polls by the Louis Harris organization showed a drastic decline in that image. When Agnew blasted the press coverage of the Nixon conduct of the war, most Americans agreed with him. And almost three-quarters of the more educated citizens told the Harris pollsters that they were most distrustful of the efforts of the press.

Perhaps there is valid reason for this. But it is likewise true that the role of the media is becoming more difficult and hazardous. In May 1971 seven reporters were ousted from a closed meeting of the Greenville, South Carolina, civil service commission. The attorney general of the state of Missouri ruled that it was proper for the Saint Louis Police Department to bar its records to the press. The *Honolulu Star-Bulletin* was denied access by the mayor to his office and to those of his department heads for almost a year. The Webb City, Missouri, personnel board barred not only the press but also the public from its regular meetings because earlier meetings had resulted in "bad publicity." In Gary, Indiana, the *Gary Post-Tribune* complained to the state superintendent of public instruction that the local school board had held secret meetings.

Why all the secrecy, these cloak-and-dagger, clandestine moves? One can hardly escape the conviction that public disclosure is feared because something is worth hiding. National security is one thing, but what is at the heart of such inanities and cover-ups among state and community bodies? Blunders, mismanagement, fraud, nepotism or just a blatant to-hell-with-the-public attitude? Whatever happened to the public's right to know?

Is the press capable of upholding that right? The challenge is becoming more difficult. According to Robert M. White II, chairman of the American Society of Newspaper Editors' committee on information, "In city after city across the nation, reporters consistently face the age-old problem of the city official, from the highest level to the lowest, who finds reasons not to reveal his mistakes, his follies, his less-than-well-done job. The same is true at the county and state level. . . . Every newspaper and news medium in the country wishes it had the quality of staff required to really dig out the misdeeds at city halls and state houses. Few of us have that much of a staff. So there is sometimes a successful kind of censorship solely because of our own inability to do that which we day to day try to do and to which we are dedicated."

## THE ROLE OF THE PRESS

Newspapers are on the defensive, worried about their role, worried about the future and, perhaps, most worried about their own self-accusations. They are looking over their shoulders at those newspapers that have gone out of business and wondering why and asking themselves if they will go out and why. But they also are looking in all directions at their critics, because that's where they are, and asking themselves why after all the years of good public service they have rendered, so many no longer believe in them. It all seems so unfair, too, since many editors and even publishers, not to mention reporters, still have that same sense of purity of purpose, the deep vein of idealism, that they started with.

What comes out in the paper is often something else, but the same sense of dedication is still there. The only problem is that newspaper publishing has become a complex affair because the signals from the public have changed and the people who work on newspapers, many of them anyway, have changed too.

If a newspaper can be likened to a person, it would be the kind of person who reacts to everything around him, becomes a receptacle of messages, you might say, before he acts. And the newspaper, too, is a message center before it turns into a performing mechanism. The *New*

*York Times*, the *St. Louis Post-Dispatch*, the *Miami Herald*—any newspaper—must wait until they see what the news is before they can decide what to do about it. There is a lapse of time or, more properly, a period of digestion. And it is that period, what happens or does not happen during it, that represents the basis for all the criticism. During that time, the newspaper must make some major decisions on whether merely to report the more important of the messages that have arrived, or to analyze them for their significance, or to analyze them objectively or to interpret them subjectively as it wishes.

If television advertisers have that crucial "thirty seconds" to sell millions, newspapers have anywhere from six hours to fifteen minutes—and sometimes even less—to make a move that will be a matter of public record a lot longer than the TV message will. Of course, there is always the opportunity to mull the decision over in subsequent editions and even days, but there can be little argument that first impressions, the first moves, are lasting and decisive with the public.

As the number of newspapers have declined, those major ones that survived have tended to soften their most salient element, whether it was sex, sensation and a preponderance of photos, or muckraking against city hall, crime and police, or a lofty, statesmanlike approach to news and editorials. To a certain extent, each newspaper that has been able to make it through the sixties and seventies has adopted some characteristics of the others while retrenching in its specialty. The reasons for this are obvious. In an effort to garner a dominant share of its market, each one has sought to round off its edges so as to be less likely to offend any important segment of that market and attract more people in the process.

Perhaps the more reasonable mix makes for a communications medium with a broader appeal but one can hardly pass this by without feeling some twinge of regret that newspapers are swiftly losing their individuality.

In New York, for example, the changes are clear. The *New York Times* publishes more crime news than it ever has, more news on sex and pornography, stretching its founder's credo, All the News That's Fit to Print, while its editorials have come down off their lofty pinnacle, sometimes obscured by gray clouds, and have made more down-to-earth and pragmatic points. The *New York Daily News*, seeking to broaden its appeal from the blue-collar and the moderate-income white-collar markets, has removed editorializing and slant from its news columns, added a variety of features, and greatly modified its hard-line conservative editorials.

Only the *New York Post*, the sole surviving afternoon sheet, appears to have remained unchanged amid the downfall of four other city newspapers in the decade, adding only columnists and some new features. Its circulation has boomed in the period, mostly because the tabloid represents virtually a monopoly for the city commuter rushing home to the five boroughs and eager to learn what has happened in city hall, sports and Wall Street. Is the lack of competition the answer? What else could it be?

In Chicago, Los Angeles, Boston, Baltimore, Dallas and elsewhere, the same trends of homogenizing the approach, or, in the case of lack of competition whether through sole ownership of several papers or the absence of others, beefing-up the product without basically changing the approach.

It is a defensive mechanism, at best. At worst, this trend has fed right into the hands of television, which has implanted itself as the most credible medium, according to surveys, and the most pervasive on news dissemination. It has been able on both a national and local level to engage in a degree of muckraking that has also helped to raise its level of confidence in the public eye.

And yet television executives freely admit that the public would be badly misinformed if it weren't for the existence of newspapers, magazines and books. There is simply a wealth and a depth of information and news in the other media that TV cannot duplicate.

If newspapers, then, as the most prevalent regional media, apparently still have durability, why are they so defensive, so uptight, so reactive rather than aggressive in their approach to the news? The rise of criticism, the factor of economics, the desire to appeal on as broad a basis as possible? Take your choice; they're all valid.

But at the same time, if you were to ask politicians, businessmen, governmental agency officials, some major figures in the world of crime, they will insist with great conviction that newspapers today are both antiestablishment and radicalized. More stories, they will tell you, are appearing that prove that the press is off on a muckraking spree. Editors and reporters have simply become antibusiness, activistic and so on, the claim goes, and there's nothing more gleeful in the newsroom than the yelps that accompany the development of yet another rough story on city hall, the police department, the White House, Wall Street and General Motors.

I think there is something to all this, but it is hardly

© 209

what it is claimed to be. Taking last things first, the yelps one might hear on the discovery of a hot story are probably more due to the satisfaction that a news medium feels when it uncovers a major development that its subjects tried to hide than it does to express an antiestablishment joy. I don't quite know if other newspapermen feel as I do, that the news we print in our newspapers really represents the tip of the iceberg and that the iceberg continues to remain submerged, but I can say with assurance that there is nothing in the business quite as personally satisfying as being able to divulge a major story that others were trying with much effort to conceal.

Is it all, then, professional satisfaction when you publish a muckraking exclusive? No, not all. There are editors and reporters who have a very big chip on their shoulders against politicians and businessmen, but their ranks are not plentiful. Most will respond to the priority of an exclusive, whether it is a muckraking story or not. But I know some editors who don't like the expression "muckraking" and seem to equate it with some sort of "yellow" journalism.

On balance, it seems to me that newspapers in general are not enterprising and investigative enough and that this represents a decline from previous years when the competitive factor in the field was much greater. There's no spur like the one that comes from another newspaper that appears on the same stands at the same time in the same city. And that, as we have learned, is simply a vanishing commodity.

If that is the case, why the exclusive disclosures (such as the Pentagon and the Vietnam Papers), the muckraking features (such as the My Lai horrors and the police corruption in New York and Chicago) and the other editorial pieces that have enraged politicians, the Pentagon, police officials and criminals?

Some of it is clear, unadulterated reportorial enterprise. But much of it, I can tell you from personal experience, represents the leaking of confidential information by sources who tend in one way or another to gain from passing on the information to a reporter. This was definitely the case in the Pentagon and Vietnam Papers and occurs in the background of many major "breakthrough" stories. Rather than existing in great numbers in the press, the real muckrakers exist on both extremes of the establishment spectrum and a competent reporter will try to cultivate sources in both camps. Each is likely to be a good source as long as he sees your byline frequently and learns to trust you enough to believe you won't reveal the source.

Chances are that behind every important exclusive story, or as it is called in the newsroom, "the news break," hides a source who will get his kicks from seeing the undisclosed story in print—preferably on the front page.

I have gotten such stories, hardly all on the front page, from unhappy former employees who were eager to tell me about shenanigans in the company they worked for; from consumer activists angry about a business that was getting away with something; from businessmen upset at an activist or activist trend; from an estranged wife who didn't mind getting her husband in a jam; from someone just plain jealous about someone else; and even from public-relations men trying to be friendly to me by passing on a tip about another company. All this has led me to spend a lot of time just trying to develop sources because that's where news tips come from.

They rarely come from a daily program of calling people you hardly know and saying, "What's new? What do you hear?" That has worked but only very occasionally. Tips come from people you have developed and sometimes they come from people who develop you. As a reporter, there's only one way to look at it. Be happy about it.

Several years ago, after writing several stories about a business merger, I began receiving telephone calls from an anonymous man who suggested that there was a situation of fraud embodied in the merger. Since the man steadfastly refused to identify himself, except to say that he was a stockholder of one of the two concerns involved, I had little respect for his information. Finally, after about six phone calls in three weeks, I told him, "I don't know why you keep calling me. Unless you tell me who you are—and give me more specifics—I'm not going to take any more calls from you."

He hung up and I never heard from him again. But in less than a year the Internal Revenue Service filed suit against the head of one of the two firms, and he eventually went to jail. Perhaps I should have listened more carefully to my anonymous caller. I assume he also called the tax people and may have alerted them to the situation. Why should he only call a newspaper?

For the last two years, I have been receiving anonymous letters mailed from a Florida city and enclosing published stories, trade-paper articles and financial tidbits about a large New York-based company. Some of the headlines or key words are encircled, accompanied by hand-written comments to the effect that I should write about the concern. The fact that I have written pieces from time to time about the firm doesn't seem to matter. The letters keep coming, probably from a stockholder who wants to see stories published that will boost the value of the stock. But I wish he (or she) would stop. I get enough junk mail.

After many years as a newspaperman, it seems clear to me that newspapers are less the initiators than messengers—conduits between those who want to see a story printed and the publishing medium itself. But newspapers should be initiators and when they perform that role, they are great and fulfill a great tradition. And I have a strong feeling that as newspapers initiate more and act less as a simple conduit, so will their viability grow.

### WORKING WITH THE COMMUNICATORS

One of the most revealing situations involving writing a simple business feature for the *Times* has centered around my experiences with a prominent businessman who heads a billion-dollar corporation. After I expressed an interest in a new program he had generated at his company to change an old shabby image of one of his subsidiaries, we had two prolonged interviews. But because of the pressure of daily developments, I was unable to write the feature

© 213

for a number of weeks. I detected some signals of impatience and frustration from my subject, a European-born administrator and a well-known but respected egocentric. But there was no overt unhappiness.

His public-relations man, however, an outside adviser, was not reluctant to call me every three or four days and ask me when the story would appear. After a while, I lost my patience and told him that it was no use bothering me since the piece would be written and appear in due course. "Is he bugging you about it?" I asked the PR man.

"No comment," he replied, "but you can use your own judgment."

Then the businessman's assistant began calling me about it.

"Is he bugging you, too?" I asked him.

"He doesn't exactly bug you," he said. "He just sort of looks you in the eye and says, 'I wonder if that story will ever appear.' "

And so it went until I had to see the businessman on another story in which his views would be combined with those of others on a major issue. At best, he would get two paragraphs. At one point in the discussion, I said, "By the way, I am still hoping to get that other story into the paper, so just be patient."

A veil seemed to drop over his face and it was immediately replaced by a flush. "My friend, did I ask you? You completely misunderstand me. Of course, it would be wonderful to have a story on me and my efforts in the *Times*—everyone aspires to such a recognition—but it doesn't matter to me. I don't need newspapers to recognize me. Whether you use it or not, we'll still be friends. We'll respect each other."

I insisted, however, in explaining why it was taking me almost two months. With an expression of pain, he allowed me to tell him about the flow of daily developments and at about midpoint, he stopped me. "Do you know what you are?" he said. "You're not American—you're a Hungarian."

"What are you talking about? I was born in the United States."

"You're definitely a Hungarian because only a Hungarian would be so stubborn. Did I even hint that you should give me an explanation? Why are you acting like a Hungarian?"

We left it that way. But the calls from his PR man and his executive assistant continued. It was obvious to me that he simply didn't want to sully his reputation by pushing for a story, the kind that "everyone aspires to." But I could just imagine the punishment he inflicted on his PR man and his assistant.

Later, I learned of yet another element in the picture. Shortly after my second interview with him, he had bragged, apparently on a grand scale, to a group of other top business executives that a favorable feature on him would soon appear in the *Times*. So he was really caught on the horns of his own self-promotion and this might have been the real prod to his devious way of pushing me.

Such are some of the machinations that sometimes—no, frequently—are involved in the relationship between the press and business. Perhaps newspaper reporting doesn't qualify one for psychoanalyzing, but I think I have run the gamut in my experiences with shook-up, neurotic types of story subjects and communicators. Here are some:

Not long ago, on the morning that a feature of mine appeared, I learned that a large firm had complained to my management that they would have been a more fitting subject of a piece than the company that I had written about. Also, the question was raised about the origin of the story. Had I worked with a public-relations man or come on it myself? I replied that I had decided to write the piece myself and contacted the head of the firm. Subsequently, I learned that the query had come from the head of a major PR agency in New York who had assured his client, the large firm, that he had impeccable contacts at the *Times*. I didn't know him personally. But when the story had run, he had irately called his impeccable source to register his bitch.

On several occasions, businessmen anxious to sell their companies at a good price have sought to have favorable stories about them appear in the *Times*. I have been able to avoid this sometimes, but not every time, because the very reasons that make a business story newsworthy are the same reasons why another firm would want to buy them. In one instance, a businessman put it to me very bluntly. "If you can do such a story," he confided, "it will raise my standing and my bank will give me the money to buy a bigger company that is up for sale. Naturally, I will be very grateful." Needless to say, I never gave him any cause to be grateful.

Then there was the international real-estate developer who offered to put me and my family up for a long weekend in a Caribbean hotel-resort only so I would become exposed to the "great" work the company was doing. They were quite clever. They suggested that as a newspaperman I would be rather interested in the secluded billionaire who had the upper floors of one of their major buildings on that island. This man, they implied, was none other than the elusive ———. I don't know if it was or even if he was on the island. I never took advantage of their "pure" generosity. But it was, as I recollect, about eight months or so before Clifford Irving surfaced with his nonautobiography of Howard Hughes.

There was the quite elderly public-relations counselor, who honestly should have known better, who invited me to lunch and then waited for some strange reason until I was chewing on a particularly big chunk of roast beef. Then he offered me $500 to do a "personality" profile on his client. I started making muffled sounds, not exactly choking but finding myself unable to chew and also clearly call him a "son-of-a-bitch." His jaw fell and he immediately countered, "Wait a minute, I'm not trying to bribe you. You don't understand me. I just mean that—" I never did find out just what he did mean except that I know what he meant.

As everyone in my business knows, there really is no such thing as a free lunch. There is always a hooker between the entrée and the dessert.

Generally, however, the routine workings between the newsmakers and the press are less colorful and more orderly. It's the exceptions, the deviousness and the feints and the double-binds, that convince the writer how careful he must be. Outside of unquestionably merited news disclosures, it is the quasi-news features, the profiles and the requests for industry "takeouts" from the industry itself about which the reporter must be most scrupulous and discriminating. There is always an ulterior motive in these suggestions, mostly one that is self-serving, so that it is wise to be suspicious about a good deal more than just the "free" lunch.

There was also the famous consumer advocate who, during an interview on a story I was preparing on a major consumerism issue, reacted to my insistence on certain facts by bluntly asking me, "Whose side are you on, anyway?" When I answered that I was on neither side as a reporter, the reaction was surprised but cooperative. And on the other side of the scale, there are the spokesmen at the many industry trade associations who willingly cooperate with the press but tell only what suits their own needs.

What does it all come down to? It's obvious, isn't it, if the press is to be free, impartial, objective and credible? It has been my experience as only one of thousands of writers on daily newspapers that a constant wariness and healthy sense of suspicion are vital. Without them, you are hanging on a shaky limb. You may miss a good story once in a while but you will probably not be sucked into a bad one.

## WHY THE "FRAGGING"?

Will the reader be served by this objective reporting, by this staunch effort to keep it all on the up-and-up, by the hard, if perhaps one-dimensional attitude of the press? And if that is to be the case, are the publishers, editors and writers on the typical daily newspaper representative enough of the reading public so that the media reflect the same level of criteria that the public has?

It seems to me that implicitly all this is a major reason for the vast criticism that has been generated against the press in recent years. If the world is in flux and the country a mirror of that and of its own internal crossfire of attitudes and conflicts, it follows that the media that report the daily happenings, television and radio as well as newspapers, will reflect all the turmoil and in so doing fall into the line of fire. Every one of those elements in our society which feels it must be vociferous in proclaiming its own attitude is convinced—and convinces itself—that the press is failing to do so. This ranges through almost the entire spectrum of American experience.

But it is when a newspaper or telecaster takes an in-depth view of the doings of one of those elements, balancing or not the positives and the negatives of the situation, that the conviction that the press is failing explodes into anger and a blast of criticism. Sometimes, it is the element itself which is reported upon, whether it is the administration, the Black Panthers, the gays or whatever, which feels maligned. Or it is other elements in conflict with the subject of the article itself, and are convinced that they have been unfairly treated.

So the accusations flow and the debate rages. The press is shallow and superficial. It is one-sided, prejudiced, antiestablishment, antibusiness, antilabor, against the equality of man, proconservative, pro-Republican, pro-Democratic, proliberal, pro-Jewish, anti-Semitic, and so on and on and on.

But the better newspapers go beyond mere objective

reporting; they analyze and interpret, too, and this infuriates the more militant of the elements in our society. If the balance of the article favors an element they abhor, the press is thereby slanting its efforts. And if it is not conversely recognizing the position of the complainant, it is surely slanting its efforts. But the worst thing of all is the occasional muckraking by the press to unearth some wrongdoing by one of the elements in society, some shenanigans that should be disclosed. That is lighting the short fuse.

To all the criticism contributing to the game of kicking the press around, the press adds its own built-in problems of conservatism, mediocrity, union security and inefficiency on the people side and archaic methods, inaccuracy and difficult deadlines on the technological side. Often, these seem to bolster the complaints—the oversimplification, the absence of follow-up, the stress on the attack and the attacker, the objective reporting minus enough interpretation, the correction that is given short shrift, the strategic errors both human and typographical and the like.

The critical blasts have led to intimidation and intimidation to incarceration and beyond that to vague threats of completely muzzling a particular medium. Where will it end?

If the press is under attack, one can only conclude that it is the people who are under attack, too, not merely one or more elements, but all of them that make up American society. The press is hardly perfect—it is probably not even as good as it used to be when there were many more media—but it is at this stage free although under attack on all sides. What would the critics substitute for it? Print media for each of the social blocs themselves? They've tried it, only no one believes in them.

In an age of false communication, double-binds, deficit catering, dishonest communicators, super PR men, all operating against a backdrop of turmoil, it is no wonder that the press is being "fragged" by more than just verbal grenades.

It is the big target. That is, next to *you*.

# IV.

## The
## Manipulated
## Society

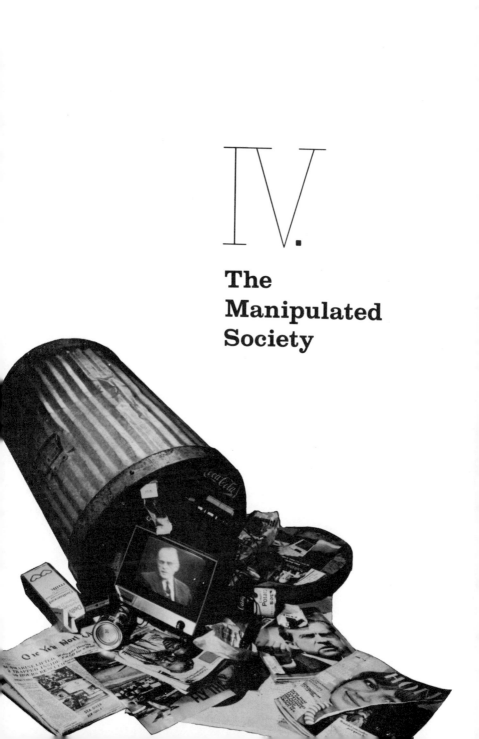

# 11.

## A Public
## Stumbling,
## as in Blind

THE WHAT-HAD-HAPPENED SYNDROME became a national trait in the early seventies. For millions of Americans who should already have become accustomed to being misled and misinformed, there seemed to be no end to the stream of deception. What had happened, they asked in the grip of a credibility crisis, to just plain integrity?

As 1972 drew to a close, the winding down of the U.S. involvement in Vietnam suddenly reverted to twelve days of massive bombing of Hanoi and Haiphong. What had happened, they wondered, to the boast of nearly consummated peace that had helped win the national elections for Richard M. Nixon just a few weeks earlier?

For some sixteen months after August 1971, federal price-and-wage controls had been working to pull in the reins on inflation. But by 1972's end, corporate profits had reached record levels while the consumer price index largely had failed to respond, recording in September one of its largest increases of the year. What had happened to the boons of the highly touted austerity program?

In the year's very last weeks, two business scandals of an unprecedented scope broke.

In what was cited as the largest stock manipulations fraud in U.S. history, the principals of the bankrupt Four Seasons Nursing Homes, stockbrokers and others were charged by the Securities and Exchange Commission with illegal stock touting—through inflating company earnings prospects—which resulted in trading of some $200 million in common stock.

The other business bombshell involved Boise Cascade Corporation, a respected major builder and producer of mobile homes, which was compelled to repay $58.5 million to unhappy buyers of land lots. In the largest out-of-court settlement ever made in California, the company was ordered to refund $24 million and spend $34.5 million to improve existing developments because it had made what the state said were illegal sales pitches to 40,000 customers.

What, one could well ask, had happened to the new responsibility and integrity of American businessmen?

If polls were already reporting increasing public dis-

enchantment, numerous new causes would increase it
further. The Watergate scandal involving political
wiretapping, the strange rapport between the International Telephone and Telegraph Company and the
Republican party, bribes and kickbacks of police and
city officials in New York and Chicago, the Clifford Irving hoax involving Howard Hughes, insider selling by
businessmen and stockbrokers, the theft of drugs under
the noses of New York police property clerks, multimil-
lion-dollar housing frauds, the bankruptcy and corporate ploys of the nation's largest railroad—the
disclosure of these in a flood of scandals had a cumula-
tive impact. It was becoming dramatically clear that the
public was being victimized, fooled and ridiculed by the
leaders of its most important institutions.

Yet these sad events at least had become part of the
public record. The revelations took them out of the area
of secrecy, of hidden perpetrations, and in so doing had
a sort of saving grace: once disclosed, the chances of a
continuing fraud on society were reduced.

But what of the deception, the policy of lies and hypocrisy, of the letting out of false lines of public information which continued unapprehended for years?
What were all the hustling, all the misrepresentation,
all the deceit, all the pervasive put-on doing to us?
Weren't we running around to accomplish things that
are basically not needed, not real, not vital?

How much of our life today represents the reaction to
manipulated behavior, to words and deeds of delusion,
all of which leads to actions that are the result of deception?

How much can we attribute some of our basic problems, whether social, spiritual or economic, to this abuse of truth and reality?

In the decades between 1950 and 1970, hundreds of billions of dollars were spent to fight one war and then another which, for many of those years, had strong, basic public support. Even when the Vietnam involvement was finally being curtailed and then the negotiations were interrupted by a resumption of heavy bombing, there was no great grass-roots reaction against it because Americans had been lured into a massive double-bind trap. The more sensitive wondered and complained, but the bulk of the population remained ambivalent on the international issue of war and peace. Yet in all those years, we also had other immense problems that cried out for attention. Crime in the streets, drug abuse, environmental pollution, widespread consumer abuses, poverty, increasing public medical needs, geriatrics care, educational requirements, the erosion of the city's inner core, inequitable tax loads and many others.

Fired on one hand by cries that shouted in effect, "Contain international communism!" and prodded on the other to "preserve national dignity" in the face of the dramatic economic and nationalistic rise of other nations, Americans were incited and herded into accepting, espousing and ultimately to resigning themselves to an Asian war. In the meantime, the problems that made America in those decades a period of traumatic disillusion for the more sensitive and more stricken were pushed aside, made to seem puny in comparison to the effort to carry on a war. And, ironically, the vast sums expended on that war were contributing to the very problems being ignored.

## The Manipulated Society

When Nixon ran for reelection in 1972 against Senator George McGovern and inundated him with an 18-million plurality, the electorate clearly showed how little it responded to the primary war issue. Lashing out on the obvious theme, to end the Vietnam conflict, McGovern badly misjudged the country's mood. So the voters rejected the South Dakotan, not at all because of concern that his election would mean a loss of national dignity by withdrawal in Asia but because they feared his domestic policies. He would be against the American style of free enterprise, he would open wide the cornucopia to the poor and the minorities, and this pitch was played with effective counterpoint by Nixon's team and his traveling surrogates.

Again the public was manipulated, sadly not because McGovern would necessarily have been a good President but because the electorate was duped to fear what his election might mean to its pocketbook while the obvious issue was carefully obscured because it was opportune to obscure it. McGovern, incidentally, would probably have turned out to be a moderate on fiscal policy. He was already veering toward it in his later speeches and policy statements in a turnabout for political reasons. But it didn't help him.

Political manipulations are an old story in America, but it is revealing to see how millions of voters can be swayed by the two elements used to sell the public what it doesn't need or want, double-binds and the playing to its deficits. Both major parties are guilty of it, and even when some clear-headed observers call attention to the deliberate persuasion, it doesn't seem to matter.

When Harry S. Truman ran against Thomas E. Dewey in 1952, the appeal by the Democrats was to portray a common man who had decisively ended a war. But if there is any truth to the fact that Dewey's mustache worked against him, it is probably more true that Truman's midwestern twang and no-nonsense ways were right for an electorate that wanted only to enjoy peace and relish calm. And his party effectively played that tune.

Much the same melody was employed to deposit General Dwight Eisenhower in the White House for eight years. The great, square-jawed father figure who had won a war but not let it turn him militant was just right for the time and the place, the Republicans trumpeted, and the voters agreed. Adlai Stevenson was a fine American in the Jeffersonian mold but he was too bright, too intellectual and perhaps too passive, the opposition hinted over and over, so that in the end the effect accumulated.

Then the Democrats were back again with their own ploy. John F. Kennedy was the perfect figure to merchandise as an antidote to two terms of disappointing, impassive paternalism. He was vital, virile and vocal, and perhaps it was time for a Catholic in the White House. He made Nixon seem old, somehow, a leering throwback to the Eisenhower era and yet ineffective and subservient to the father figure. Reviving the "New Frontier" battle cry, Kennedy squeaked through by a margin of only 119,450 votes out of 69 million cast. When Lyndon Johnson succeeded the assassinated Kennedy in 1963, he followed the liberalism of his predecessor and raised a banner for the "Great Society." He easily swamped Senator Barry Goldwater of Arizona in 1964 as the Democrats successfully played on the fears of

Americans that the Republican contender would push the country to the far Right and engulf it in a class and racial struggle.

But Johnson withdrew in 1968 from a second campaign, having surrendered credibility because of the Vietnam war, government scandals and inflation. Nixon, the professional loser who had won with Eisenhower and then lost because of him, became the beneficiary of the disaffection which Johnson had left on the voters. In one of the most effective—if not chilling—Madison Avenue campaigns in recent presidential electioneering, Nixon was perfumed, packaged, beribboned and peddled to the public as the herald to a better, cleaner, more reliable time. The pitch was, "This Time Vote Like Your Whole World Depended Upon It!" He defeated Hubert H. Humphrey, the former vice-president whom the Democrats had summoned up, and Nixon committed himself to end the war with "dignity."

But four years later, with the Vietnam war still under way after 50,000 Americans had been killed under three Presidents, Nixon gave McGovern a shellacking. Obviously, if the nation wasn't unduly concerned about the war, it was more concerned over the hazards of change, a change that the Republicans had carefully emblazoned with warning signs. But in view of the double meanings and the failure to carry out pledges on peace and inflation on the part of the President, it may well be that the public simply bought his bland assurance that "We are giving government back to the people . . . because people want better government, not bigger government."

Came 1973, however, and Americans were worried

that they had been deceived once more. And yet, even though demonstrations were planned and protesting advertisements were taken on the resumption of heavy bombing, one could hardly report that people were pouring out on the streets to express their horror. So it was obvious that Americans had been taken in by a massive double-bind.

Every American president in recent history has been a skilled deceiver, some more than others. Overselling himself to capture the highest office, each found that he had promised more than he could deliver. Somehow we have come to perpetuate a myth that the average citizen knows and accepts this political fact of life. But this is only a myth. The opposition party usually seizes the opportunity to exploit an excess of failure for its own purposes and in the process Americans are again manipulated. The right to mandate such failure out of authority has gradually been taken away from the electorate, which strangely, perhaps, in an age of so-called sophistication and abundant communications, hasn't quite come to recognize this theft of one of its most basic privileges.

But then the average person is no obstacle to the predatory image maker or, more importantly, his client or sponsor, the power seeker.

If America still remains a business economy, which it is, we have also come passively to regard the reality that corporate structure and its profit motive offer a near-perfect climate for treachery, deceit and false communications. Under the pressures and priorities of corporate goals, freedom of expression has joined the erosion of the electoral mandate as an increasingly vanished cause.

In 1971 and 1972, two years when thousands of businesses enforced belt-tightening, expense-cutting programs, many employees were released in staff reductions. It is hardly conjecture but fact that the most likely candidates for firing, everything else being equal, were those who spoke too freely or too unwisely or protested too much the corporate yoke. And, at the same time, if top-management men had wanted to show their disdain for their communications aides, they took the occasion to do so in their austerity efforts. Many a public-relations man was let go, many a PR agency was chopped in fees or let go while advertising and sales-promotion men and their assistants also became expendable.

The hypocrisy, double-binding and bogus communications that are such a great element in the corporate scene have already been covered in detail. As a long-time close observer of business, however, I can't help wondering what has happened and what will happen further to the faith and the confidence that so many people used to have toward their business superiors and even toward the goals of constant growth and profit appreciation.

I can't leave at this juncture without reporting, probably with malice, a recent incident which involved a troubled corporate chief and a public-relations "statesman" to whom he went for advice.

Ignoring his own PR staff and a respected outside PR counselor, the business executive sought out the semiretired public-relations expert and explained the problem. It revolved around the fact that the diversified manufacturing company was earning less and less in the last few years despite its annual sales of several hundred million dollars. Soon management would face an annual meeting that would probably find several major stockholders upset, ornery and very vocal.

"I'd love to divert the attention of those big shareholders at the meeting," said the businessman. "What should I do?"

The elder PR man put his venerable head in his hands and thought and thought. Finally, he looked up. "Hire a bunch of chorus girls and put on a show at the meeting," he said.

The tycoon nodded nervously. "Yes, but what should I do about my profits?" he asked.

The expert thought and thought and then he had it. "Stop issuing quarterly financial reports," he said. "That ought to help."

The businessman swallowed painfully and asked, "But what the hell should I do with my board of directors? They're starting to give me trouble."

That really gave the expert reason to pause. Ultimately, he came up for air. "Fire the whole bunch," he said. "Then go outside and hire the first ten men you meet, no matter who they are. That ought to end your troubles with the board."

That, I deceive you not, is a true story. But it is not quite all. As the businessman staggered out, the PR man added, "Just a minute. To show you how confident I am that it will work, I'll bet my fee on it."

The surprised and still-shaken businessman agreed and left. Although desperate, he was sensible enough not to put into effect any of the three suggestions. But he sent word back to the PR man that the plan hadn't worked. The ruse didn't pay off. He never got the fee back.

In more recent years, one of business's most flagrant put-ons has been its concern and professed action on environmental protection. Much of it amounted merely to advertising, calling attention to the environmentally conscious company, and most of that turned out to be misleading and even blatantly false claims.

Late in 1971, a New York-based nonprofit organization, the Council on Economic Priorities, reported that ecology ads have consistently carried false and misleading statements. Added the CEP, "Even if the ads are entirely honest in fact and implication, many environmentalists, businessmen and even communications executives question whether the millions of dollars spent by the companies for self-aggrandizement wouldn't be better invested in pollution control equipment or research and development."

Again, in other words, a cosmetic, superficial effort, more often than not, is the means businessmen take to solve a problem that has surfaced to embarrass them.

In surveying all 1970 issues of *Time, Business Week* and *Newsweek,* the CEP survey found 289 pages of environmental advertising by 27 firms costing about $6 million. Said the report, "The five industries responsible for well over half the advertising were the same ones identified in a May 1971 study by the McGraw-Hill economics department as having the biggest clean-up job to do." The five were the electrical utilities, iron and steel, petroleum, paper and chemical industries. And the research group found that six out of seven papermakers who did environmental advertising were those found to have distinctly unimpressive environmental records.

Of course, the public had its own reasons to scoff at such claims, that is, if it connected them with the streams of yellow, blue and brown smoke rising from many an industrial smokestack. The horizon over many a city—and lately over the suburbs—shows the by-products of those stacks, a rainbow stain in all shades of brown, black and awful.

Not as evident to the public, perhaps, was a dismaying report by the National Water Commission, a federal agency which charged late in 1971 that not the public but the Bureau of Reclamation, the Army Corps of Engineers and numerous powerful private interests benefit out of all proportion to what they pay from federally financed waterways, irrigation systems and flood-control efforts. It was charged in the same report that many of these developments have been detrimental to the environment. Something like $8 billion of federal expenditures in recent years have been poured into stream channelization, diversion of rivers, irrrigation and flood control, but still flood damage has continued to grow, leading to loss of life and property.

How well and how sincerely were the federal regulatory and other agencies upholding the public interest by curbing abuses? Not well and not very sincerely, for most Washington agencies are industry-oriented, often ignoring the consumer need and not even being very sensitive to the resulting criticism. Could the Pentagon effectively defend the vast expenditure of $190 million a year to peddle defense and the need to fight communism abroad? Yet it bristled along with the Nixon Administration when the Columbia Broadcasting System presented its February 1971 documentary, "The Selling of the Pentagon," a revealing program but one which CBS admitted could have been even harder hitting.

The Pentagon wasn't alone in carrying forth an expensive promotion campaign. In 1972, a House subcommittee survey disclosed that 76 federal agencies signed almost 300 contracts with Madison Avenue for advertising and other image-building services from 1970 through 1972, spending a total of $80 million.

Not quite a year earlier, the Federal Communications Commission, in three separate decisions, declined to expand its limited role to police false advertising. Claiming that the Federal Trade Commission was specifically created by Congress to deal with that problem, the FCC spurned requests that it adopt a federal code of advertising practices by broadcasters, that it apply the "fairness doctrine" to allegedly deceptive toy advertisements and that it revise license applications in such a way as to identify applicants' procedures to prevent deceptive advertising. The agency's reluctance to move into what were obviously vital areas led a dissenting commissioner, Nicholas Johnson, to accuse his colleagues of a "do-nothing attitude."

But then the FCC's do-nothingness, at least as far as the public was concerned, was no different than that of most other federal agencies. As consumerists claimed in 1972 when the proposed legislation for a Consumer Protection Agency languished under a filibuster in Congress, as well as White House and agency opposition, it was additional evidence that the consumer needed advocates in government. Industry was quick and eager to present itself at hearings before the agencies, but who countervailed, who supported and defended the consumer's position in such hearings? Not the government, not business and, except for a few, not the elected representatives.

While I have concentrated on the deceptive methods

used by three elements in our communications matrix —government, business and the professional communicators—I feel a need also to cover in very brief terms some other types of misrepresentations practiced on the American public. I refer to sales promotion and to "society" promotion, if I can put it that way. Both are important ingredients in the array of gimmickry that is constantly being cranked against the public.

At the risk of forever being damned by the sales promotion people—and I'll take that risk—I am convinced that some of their methods are anticonsumer and possibly wasteful to business. Premium promotion, for example, often represents a "something for nothing" aspect but it is nothing but a come-on. Not only are the toys, books, plastics, gadgets and such which the consumer gets as a premium relatively worthless, but they cause the public to load up on packaged goods that it otherwise wouldn't buy. The same principle of unfair consideration to the consumer and undue benefit to the sponsor applies to lotteries or games of chance offered the public by some media, toilet goods and food companies. Fortunately, the Federal Trade Commission not long ago compelled sponsors of such games to award all the prizes they advertised and to publish lists of awardees to prove it.

Trading stamps, too, are another form of promotional come-on, enticing customers to buy more than they need in the hope of getting something for nothing. Retailers who drop trading stamps generally lower their prices about 3 percent because they no longer have to pay for the stamps. But consumers who save stamps to redeem them for "premiums" do not realize that they are redeeming stamps for merchandise tagged at the full list price. And list prices today are no longer being maintained by retailers in many categories of goods. So what is the stamp-saving public really getting?

By "society promotion" I mean the exploitation of the "beautiful people"—which I am convinced is yet another pervading sham practiced by communicators short on creativity. In many media and in numerous types of business, cultural and charitable affairs, the foisting of the beautiful people, the jet set, is aimed at impressing the middle-income person, the woman particularly, and the would-be climber or dreamer-aspirant that the message, the medium and the event are significant because of the presence or participation of famous names bandied about in the gossip columns.

If one examines the fleeting presences, the superficial attention most of these people tend to give the matter at hand before they get briefly involved in another, it is fairly easy to see the hand of an eager PR man (or sharp-eyed PR gal) in the process. Anyone who thinks he or she must accept the example, the participation or even the endorsement of the beautiful person (many of them really aren't) in a society promotion is very obviously deluding himself or herself. The slavish imitation or acceptance of superficial glamour is merely proof that someone who lacks self-confidence is swallowing another form of put-on. The beautiful people themselves know this and insist on some sort of recompense for their participation, be it money, publicity or the promise of a future favor. While they crave imitation for its flattery value, they laugh at and ridicule those who imitate them. They know, they know. Yet we continue to be inflicted with the society promotion in a temptation to the snobbish, silly and simpering attitude of many of us when it is nothing more than a harmless exercise in vanity and quid pro quo.

There is both a great difference and a distinct similarity between promotional gimmickry and the illusion cast by the promotion of the beautiful people. Both, however, have the same goal as far as their recipients are concerned. They are ploys intended to build a smokescreen between the public and things as they are.

### SUMMING UP THE EFFECTS

In the meantime, while so many of their vital needs were being given the back of the hand, and phony promises and widespread deceit were forcing a new set of value criteria on them, what was happening to many Americans?

In earlier chapters, I have described this in some detail in connection with specific causes. But the totality of what has been perpetrated on much of the American public might be put together at this point:

I. *We accept shoddy products and inflated services because of false stimuli.* Many, many Americans find themselves today to be the unwilling buyers of products and services that they do not need, want, benefit from or enjoy. Product deterioration and obsolescence continues unabated in a wide range of major items—automobiles, clothes, furniture, many appliances, homes, home furnishings—while servicing most of these items remains inadequate, difficult and expensive. Although as a business writer I already know that businessmen can combat this contention effectively through a combination of PR tactics and a plethora of convincing statistics, I suggest that my claims are no mere oversimplification. As prices rise at a rate of 5 percent to 8 percent annually, quality and durability of products diminish each year. Retailers blame this on manufacturers and manufacturers blame it on an erosion of responsibility by assembly-line workers, truckmen, shippers, et al., but the unvarnished fact is that quality control in manufacturing has not been given the stress in our country that it has in recent years in Japan, West Germany, England and Italy.

Instead, because of its merchandising clout, we have been subjected to the lure of fashion, style, speed, color, sound, horsepower, gadgetry and miniaturization, rather than being given our due on product performance and durability. The argument that our gross national product would suffer irretrievably if we surrendered the principle of obsolescence is, I submit, a claim that amounts to superficiality, laziness and simple softheadedness. Who can say that it is not just as likely that our GNP would jump if better engineering, greater honesty in manufacturing, more quality inspection and more integrity were built into our new products?

Services, too, have involved much deception. Travel, medical, financial, insurance and other services have been sold to us by a play on our deficits, our fears that without guarantees of ease, convenience and security we would be subjected to the misfortunes of ever-rising costs, unexpected illness and accidents and indigent old age. I don't mean to knock all services but merely to point out that we get precious little from most of them —for which we pay increasing sums both directly and indirectly. We are simply being oversold and overmerchandised on the benefits of many services, particularly on many forms of insurance. The strictures, for example, practiced by automobile insurers against those insured, such as automatic cancellation when the policy must be enforced, are indefensible.

But how many of us have become sufficiently aware of all these violations of public need? If Nader, Rosenthal, Proxmire, Moss, Myerson, Furness, Magnuson and all the other consumer advocates of various degrees of effectiveness have called our attention to it, relatively few Americans have taken it to heart or, for that matter, have even listened attentively. Instead, we have behaved as though the consumerists were agitators, somehow un-American, and as a result we have regarded them with some suspicion. True, they sometimes are strident, overdo their arguments and occasionally show a lack of understanding of specific situations. But what successful or aggressive contender on a significant issue doesn't? Yet, even here, the theory of overcompensation, of demanding 150 percent correction in order to obtain 75 percent or even less, hasn't quite worked, although the consumerists have pushed government and business into a number of reluctantly granted concessions. Among these are the Automobile Safety and the Consumer Safety Agency bills. But much remains to be done.

We still need a consumer-protection agency on a federal level to represent us in all consumer matters and a better protection range of consumer needs. Among them are more truthful food labeling, a uniform system of food grading, better nutritional information on labels, a federal unit-pricing law on food, a performance-life-disclosure bill, an appliance life-dating statute and protection against such of the sleazier merchandising stunts as promotional games.

2. *Much of our behavior has been wrong or misguided because of false stimuli.* What do we want most? It may be the last thing we are getting. All of us crave two basic things—happiness fulfillment and peace of mind. But we are getting neither because we have been lulled into a false behavior pattern that has come as a substitute for both fulfillment and emotional calm. Through a combination of double-talk, double-binds, deception and delusion, we have accepted the palliative that intentions and promises are tantamount to the rewards that elude us.

In all pursuits, the average American seeks satisfactions that come only in small doses, whether it is a solution to his own immediate problems of family security, career enjoyment, neighborhood stability, spiritual calmness or national dedication. Lacking any consistent pattern of satisfaction or gratification, we should be groping toward remedies, toward an easing of irritation and dissatisfaction, but even this is denied us. The reason is that we have been tranquillized into an acceptance of things as they are, at least the semblance of things as they are that has been foisted on us. Even our classic American sense of right and wrong has been carefully and systematically chipped away and soon may even be stolen from us.

We have insulated ourselves and our families from many of the problems that vitally affect us now and will do so even more in the future. It isn't necessary to list them all, except to mention such basic unresolved issues as inflation, education, civil rights, ecology protection, medical needs, product reliability and consumer protection, tax inequity.

Doped by false security, prodded into fears by a flaming of his frustrations, stimulated to accept the pattern of things as they are by empty although glamorous promises, the average American hurries to pursue his daily life with no more than an occasional glance or frown at the significant matters that he senses about him. His involvement in them is reduced; he has succumbed to the subterfuge that things are probably a lot better than they seem. Forgotten, ignored or crammed into some sort of memory abyss is the realization that agitation in America over two centuries has produced benefits once thought highly radical.

We spend hours each week watching the sales pitches on television and the accompanying pallid entertainment which is also intended to sell us, and we sink into a national indulgence, an amiable bleary-eyed jesting that says in effect, "Why bitch about it? It's free, that's all there is and what can you expect, anyway?" The self-deception is obvious. None of it is free. We are paying for it in government subsidies and in the higher cost of products and services, and there certainly can be a much better quality of merchandising and certainly much better entertainment. And we can demand better because we had it in the early years of television before sponsor greed and the shenanigans of the professional communicators took over. Are mediocrity, inanity and deception the price of progress? Aren't we accepting that premise? If that's progress, maybe we ought to go back to the hand-cranked phonograph.

We show the same kind of lassitude not only on the quality of things we buy but also on the foolish and deceptive manner in which they are often sold to us. Hypnotized into acceptance that the false, niggardly, simpering approach and the blatant appeals to what are not our needs are all that we may expect, we accept them and suffer. We suffer, too, the arrogant and disinterested ways in which we are treated by sales clerks, mechanics, servicemen and others as if that were all we are entitled to. After all, some of us are sales clerks and mechanics and servicemen, too, and we know how terrible it is, how humiliating and insufferable to serve the public, and so completely understanding that, we suffer in virtual silence.

The point is that we seem to have lost our antennae of suspicion, our traditionally low boiling point and our aggressive push for what is ours. The hustling, the deception, the spurious fears are preventing us from realizing that we are being had—and had on so many fronts.

Am I beginning to become strident? I hope so.

3. *Wrong stimuli are fed by deliberate confusion (double-binds) and by our frustrations (deficits).* I won't belabor this at this point since it has already been discussed in detail. All I want to say here is that while I think that the use of these two stratagems is widespread among all our basic institutions and by many communicators, it really doesn't matter how much of it is

deliberate or how much is instinctive. The application of double and confusing messages and the play to our frustrations represent formalized methods used by politicians on all levels of government and by many businessmen. But among the communications professionals, it seems to me that the methods are informal or instinctive and reflect a dependence on scare tactics that have become integral after long years of successful use. I doubt that many of these individuals or others in leadership positions even know what the term double-bind means. But that doesn't prevent them from using it.

4. *Grand deception and misguided behavior lead to a diminution and a diversion of our own values and the acceptance of the values of others.* This, too, has been discussed in detail earlier. Nevertheless, in the following chapter I have attempted to portray in fictional terms how a man loses his own set of values and accepts those that are forced on him by deceivers and their deceptions. Pursued to its ultimate, which I contend it is and will be, this pattern can have only one conclusion.

Why have so few of us been able to resist the pull on our beliefs and the strain on our convictions? Happiness and security have become illusory for many because our views of both those states have been warped to suit the criteria of others. If financial success has been a goal, it has been robbed from us by a huge drain on the value of the dollar, high taxes and the inept uses of public money. If peaceful existence is a goal, it seems that it is now possible to have peace in the midst of carrying on a military campaign. If joy in living in a heterogeneous society is a goal, it's obvious that that very heterogeneity is being used as a weapon to fire our frustrations. If enjoying the benefits of a highly sophisticated technology, and the "good life" that should emanate from it, is a goal, the guile and the decoys that are involved in merchandising all sorts of products and services certainly provide a rude awakening. If you still think your home is your castle and your objective is to keep it that, make sure you leave your door locked, chained and secured at night. And don't wander out alone at night, either. Yet we are told that crime is on the down trend now and, besides, how can you trust the statistics?

5. *We have become desensitized and callous.* Implicitly believing that all is well, the one-dimensional attitude may be causing us really to believe in nothing. Pervasive delusion, in other words, is making us nonreactive to many things that we should believe in and be concerned about. The loss of credibility not only in our communications elements but also in our institutions is the direct result of our being fed a constant diet of false information. Even our borrowed values are unable to sustain the big gap between what we are told and what we see. But how much are we really seeing? Aren't we a public stumbling, as in blind?

6. *The desensitizing of our emotions and the theft of our values have pushed us into playing a personal game of deception.* The home used to be the cave that one could slink to and lick his wounds. But even that is going. The assaults on our basic instincts, inflicted over a period of years, have an adverse effect on our personal relationships on all levels of intimacy. And the resulting personal deceptions have created family and human problems which otherwise might never have developed.

© 247

7. *The result of all this is that in many ways how we live and what we do represents an enforced fantasy.* If it is true that our values are subverted, if basic instincts and impulse are altered through confusion and contrived fears, if personal relationships are being torn apart, if our behavior is falsely stimulated and if our emotions have been tranquillized, then it would appear logical that what remains is a type of fantasy existence. We haven't yet come into a state of pure fantasy, perhaps, but we have given up much of reality for a never-never world, where fantasy is shunting aside reality. Soon, if it all continues, we may be ready for the ultimate delusion.

# 12.

## The
## Ultimate
## Delusion

IT IS 7:08 on a typical morning in the life and times of a man preparing to become a jellybean, the morning a bit grayer than gray, as he noticed looking out the window with bleary eyes and not any particular desire to face what is outside.

He is the average man. He is thirty-eight years old, about five feet, eight inches tall, weighs about 165 pounds, has an average number of natural and attained scars and blemishes with an accumulated number of lesions on his nervous system and bears the knowledge of a series of internal conflicts he doesn't fully understand. He is about to struggle with his daily routine of

© 249

inserting himself into that segment of the general consciousness that is his life.

Between those waking moments and breakfast, he is
only faintly conscious of, but sensitive to, the reality
that something is wrong with the world. Vaguely, he
knows that he lives in a society where deception is the
rule and truth the exception. He can no longer trust the
politician, the businessman, his employer; he is not
even sure he can get the time of day from his friends.
And as far as his family is concerned, there are times he
is not certain he is involved in any meaningful conversation with them anymore.

Half an hour later, he feels better. With the removal
of sleep from his muscles and bones, the pure zest of life
has reentered him, and the sight of his wife and one of
his children (one of whom lives away) has worked the
daily miracle again: the emotional and physical sense
of being alive.

He has munched some dry cereal (minus any real
nutritive value), chewed through some low-calorie toast
(machine-made, virtually tasteless and really not very
low in calorie content), and sipped a cup and a half of
coffee (high in caffeine). Through it all, he waved
vaguely to his school-bound daughter, listened with
some impatience and indulgence to his wife's comments (she will be lonely, after all, most of the day) and
read his home-delivered newspaper (the news is the
same as yesterday's, only a day worse). The radio on the
windowsill has chattered away with the same barrage
of political maneuverings that lately has seemed
remote to him, with war and foreign news that has increasingly assumed the monotonous tone of a type-

writer, with the warnings about higher prices and less take-home pay that he ignores.

After a peck on his wife's cheek that neither he or she will remember seconds later, he is out the door and grinding a two-year-old car that didn't even start right the day he bought it and has become more sluggish since. He parks it in a commercial lot along the railroad's right of way, paying twice as much as he thinks he should. He joins a throng; the train arrives and the doors trundle open. For perhaps the umpteenth thousandth time, he is swept along almost helplessly in a mindless group boarding a commuter train. He blocks and feints his way to a seat, grins helplessly at the guy he beat out for it and leans back out of breath.

He is on his way and, sensing some vague tremors at being trapped in a life that he didn't create or for that matter even control, he opens his attaché case for a book, magazine or office memo to ease the forty-five-minute trip. Nothing seems very inviting so he surrenders to a type of cataleptic state made up of a slight headache, concern and sleepiness. At more or less 9:15, he is regurgitated along with the mob into a vast station, cold and forbidding. Moments later, fighting off a vague harassment, he has almost but not quite inserted himself into his world. He is now a company man in an impersonal company.

Between 9:35 A.M. and 5:30 P.M. when he reverses the process, his mind becomes a refuse can of unwanted, undigested thoughts and scraps of thoughts. After some real advancement, why has he remained on the same company assignment so long? (Does the rut that he has been compelled to dig for himself increasingly hide his visibility?) Why was he so hot in the early years and so taken for granted in more recent ones? (Is it likely that loyalty and hard effort are somehow being held against him?) Why has his salary growth rate been so stunted, why are taxes so high, why does the stock in the employee purchase plan fail to rise? (Is there something in the makeup of the economy which militates against people on a fixed income?) Why is he always in debt— doesn't the credit system make him not so much a more fulfilled American as an American with a lot of unfulfilled debts? In that gray mood he can't help wondering, too, what has happened to his home life. Why has his marriage turned flat, what has happened to the yeast in it? What has happened to the heat in his love for her? What has happened to the love in his heat? Aren't the kids, little as they are, beginning to pull away from them, the younger ones losing their sensitivity and attentiveness, the oldest one not even listening? (Do children *know* how little their parents know?) Why, while he was still so young, did he begin settling for an unexciting, humdrum existence? Or was it that just like everyone else he compromised with life because one can't control one's present, much less one's future? Or is it all just a matter of finding a crevasse covered on all three sides into which one can conveniently hide? But why hide?

Staring out the window as the train hurtles back across the countryside, he decides his rotten mood is due to a change in the weather, now more gray than bright, and to the occasional, unpitying self-scrutiny that any man still alive must feel. The conclusion brings a faint, not unhappy smile to his lips, but he gathers that it was something else that troubled him but what it was he doesn't know. Perhaps it was just that he had lost himself somewhere between home and job. Someone or something had gotten him off the track while he was on the train and maybe it was even he, both the victim and the culprit. . . .

*In a fragmented society, insecurity, confusion and turmoil lie close to the surface. Status drive, social and economic rivalry, class and political competition and fear of losing one's stability have become the basic stimuli. Much of these are due to abuses of truth and reality which act to transform the behavior of many. To repeat, the average individual, often unaware of the threat, presents no obstacle to the predatory image maker.*

*If the mouse in a maze offers a subject of amazement and delight to the psychologist, the humans who run by false stimuli offer an even more toothsome subject to those who may be intrigued by the simple but strange relationship of cause and effect.*

Prenatally, he had begun life without blemish or interference, the warm pleasure of his surroundings never quite leaving him from the first instinctive moment of fetal consciousness. Later, outside in the imperfect world, he was never quite as certain of himself, at least that was his conviction when buffeted by unexpected attacks on his self-confidence. And then, all through his life, there was always that overhanging question about what was ahead for him. As a child, he would ask, even more serious and pink-cheeked than before, "Mother, what do you think I ought to be when I grow up?" Her reply was disappointing, "Whatever you want to be, my son, whatever pleases you, that you will be." His father: "You'll know for sure when you get there, boy." His teacher: "It's a matter of inclination and aptitude. Don't decide prematurely. As you mature, you will develop inclinations and aptitudes."

Only it didn't work out that way. He grew up in the post-depression when all was practicality, when the stress was on getting a job, any job; and quickly, before he knew it, he was in the armed services in a localized Asian war in which the stress was on survival. So if he developed an inclination, it was on staying alive and his aptitude turned out to be that, too. But he floundered. Thus he lost his first important value: confidence in the wisdom of his elders.

The meaninglessness of the war, which ended in a stalemate, dawned on him, but he submerged it under the blast of patriotic music and mottoes that attended those years and spilled over into the second Asian war. Confused by the disparity of his inner doubts and his outward, positive reaction to the battle calls of his three years of army service, he lost his second major value: confidence that the government spoke for him or worried over any one individual's well-being. He did not quite articulate it that way, perhaps, being a shy young man, and he kept the question to himself, but it recurred and he just swallowed the hollow thought. After all, he asked himself, why should the Commander-in-Chief and the Congress worry just about him? But as he grew older, as his doubts increased, he said it out loud, "Why the hell shouldn't they?"

He entered college, his tuition paid by the grateful government, and soon shifted to business administration. He did so because in the world of commerce it seemed for the first time in his life that he saw some means of organization, a logical structure, a natural, equationlike progression of A + B = C. He did well in his studies, even though he held a part-time job. If anything bothered him in those relatively happy years, it was his irksome questioning of the profit goal, whereas what he had envisioned in the business pursuit was a sort of beauty and justice in numbers and in the synergistic efforts of people. But it got worse after graduation when he entered a large corporation. The merits of profits on society were clear to him, but after a few years, and despite an upward movement in his career, he found to his surprise that the corporation was least of all interested in people fulfillment, or for that matter in the beauty of any kind of logic except in that accidental logic that built a steady progression of the numbers at the bottom line.

Nonetheless, he did well, perhaps because when he had lost the other two important values he submerged the erosion of a third one: his confidence in the business establishment. He attempted to convince himself with, "How do I know I would do better if I were the top man?" That was a lie, he knew. He knew it even more so when several people he respected received shabby, if not cruel treatment after long years of service and dedication to the corporation.

Through friends, he met first one girl, then another, and finally—her. She was cool, wide-eyed and ingenuous, intriguing him in part because she still possessed

© 255

most of the ideals that he seemed to be losing. Her zest invigorated him and her milky skin stirred him. When they were married, he felt that a new stage had opened for him, even a new world. He could not quite get over the fact that such a beauty had elected to align her life with his, and for several years this did more to raise his spirits and build his confidence than anything else that happened. That is, until their children came along, and they seemed in their infancy, childhood and adolescence to be startling extensions of her.

He was a happy man.

*When a man becomes a father, some chemical change causes him to reexamine many things that he believes in, to reassess his values. It is as if one must, in the face of added responsibilities, make an audit of one's moral inventory and basic attitudes about life. In other words, if one has reached the stage of becoming father and family head, relying until then on one set of values, it would seem that the new role might require some updating of those values. In a way, it is like an actor assuming a new part in the same play, thereby necessitating either major or subtle changes in the setting to suit the new personality on the stage.*

*But there is a problem in this. It is more difficult for a man to revise his values than for a stage setting to be altered. Each of us is the sum of our experiences over many years and of our reactions to the world we live in. Some of those reactions dig deep and notch themselves on the memory mechanism. No matter how much you try, the most deeply embedded beliefs remain unshakable. In the effort to jar loose the entrenched values, each additional reaction of the type that caused that un-flappable conviction merely seems to solidify its effect.*

*It all depends, of course, on how much one can with-stand the onslaught of change. But—ask yourself—if the occasional raindrop that falls for a thousand years on a rock to no effect were increased to a torrent and even then cut only a tiny scratch on the rock's surface, what will a lifetime of lies, deception, false messages and misguided behavior do?*

And so the average man tried. He tried to reevaluate his convictions. As he gazed with growing amazement and deepening attachment at his children, as he studied every move his wife made and marveled at her grace and devotion, he pondered the elements of cynicism that had infected him in recent years. Somewhat with-drawn from others, he tried at times to express himself openly so that he would not be really shy and so he told his wife:

"You know, honey, I've been thinking a lot lately. Like everyone else I've gotten bruised over the years and I've become kind of pessimistic about some things. It all boils down to the fact that I've lost respect for or confi-dence in some of the basic things—the wisdom of older people, the sincerity of government, the so-called 'lack of soul' of business. But what bothers me is how the hell can I be a good father to these kids when I'm so turned off on important values? Sooner or later, as they get older, they'll start asking me questions about these things. I'll either have to lie or influence them wrongly. The natural thing is to let them find out for themselves, isn't it?"

His wife's expression, which had turned from surprise to dismay as he spoke, now switched again. She
smiled confidently and said with assurance, "You'll
know what to do when the time comes. You always do.
I'm not worried one bit whether you'll be a good father
to the children. Just don't forget about me." And she
kissed him on the forehead.

So he was on his own again. Why was it that everyone
was so damned understanding and certain that the answers were all there within him when he would need
them? The truth was that he had no answers. All he had
was a deepening loss of faith. Was he more shaken,
more neurotic, more lost than his friends and contemporaries—or just maybe more sensitive?

Oddly enough, his wife's overwhelming confidence in
him was especially painful and disappointing. What
was wrong with him? Everyone seemed to think he did
well on his own, but inwardly he knew that he was in
serious trouble. As the family grew, he withdrew even
more. Not much more, but he refused now to volunteer
his innermost thoughts because they might expose him
to his children and his wife. He couldn't quite stand up
to her when he was losing his confidence in so many
things.

Disappointed and hurt, his wife took over a more
dominant role, becoming both a full-time mother and a
part-time father. And, correspondingly, his warmth for
her cooled. As he rounded forty, he found it impossible
to change himself or the situation. He had made his
terms with life, such as they were, and his value scale
had settled at balance. There was in this resolution of
his uncertain world some element of assurance for him.

Sometimes, at night, though, after he had looked in on the kids and lay in bed listening to his wife's regular breathing, he would wonder why he couldn't behave like some of his friends who managed to have a much more assured, more positive demeanor than they really felt. As one warned him, "Wear your heart on your sleeve, man, and you're done for sure." What was so demeaning about maintaining a hard shell, a confident front? But he couldn't.

Yet his career prospered. Despite the turmoil that roiled in him, he became a department head, an administrator of a large group of people; his salary rose yearly by big increments and at forty-six he was a vice president. But he knew that as he got closer to the top, his eventual exposure also came closer; and so his cynicism grew. It became an effort at times to hold himself in, to control the objections that welled up in him. Can you sit by quietly and smile, he wondered, when you see numerous illegalities perpetrated by your own employer, when you witness hypocrisy, participate in racial tokenism, practice discrimination in sex and age, share in unfair trade practices, assist in withholding information and in general say the opposite of what you know and claim to know what you don't?

He did.

*So what, then, is success? What is composure? What is confidence? What is happiness? The answer to all four is the same—success, composure, confidence and happiness are not what one wears on his sleeve but what one feels inside. It's not hard to compromise with life, it's easy, in fact; but it's infinitely harder to com-*

*promise with the most intense feelings you have if they are continuously jarred by outside pressures. Either you bow to them or you change inside. Whoever heard of a jellybean having a nervous breakdown?*

As the children grew up, he mellowed. When his oldest son was summoned to the now decade-old second Asian war, he swallowed the pain. When the younger one found his way into a youthful activist group, it was somewhat easier to smile tolerantly against the pain because he was getting used to it. When his daughter became a teen-aged terror, fighting and snarling about everything possible, he felt not so much pain as intermittent irritation. By then, his wife had dried up in a sense, her grace having become awkward, as if the loss of love had withered her and her devotion was just a badge that she flaunted.

Turning philosophical, his irritations became passive and only very occasionally would he outwardly fume against things—for instance, the oversell and the overclaim that he understood so well as a businessman and a consumer. Somehow, though, his ire rose at governmental deception—he was, after all, personally involved through his son. He hoped that his other son's waywardness would run its course. It didn't. Youth is always the easiest mark for the one who professes to bear the conscience of society, the fanatic, and so the father began to lose even his idealism over the rights of the forgotten and the downtrodden. Or, if he didn't exactly surrender all of it, he learned that along with everything else it was best to sweep it under the rug of his indifference.

As he rounded fifty, it dawned on him that he would be unable to satisfy his lifelong ambition of finding some way of inserting himself into a world of his choice. He was not so far gone that he could delude himself that the carefully guarded, self-sufficient enclave that he had become represented any kind of happy rapprochement with life. It was obviously just an escape.

But, he asked himself, how can one "insert" oneself into a world when life as it is has no insertable possibilities, no crevasses, no overhangs, no caves? And surrendering his last real value he built his own crevasses, his own overhang, his own cave. In them he was finally able to hide from everything and everyone, even ultimately, it seemed, to hide from himself. He had found his perfect world, emotionless, inviolate, jellybeanlike—nothing.

# 13.

## Individuality
## and Identity,

*or, Will the Real* You
*Please Stand Up?*

I have ever hated all nations, professions and communities,
and all my love is towards individuals. . . . But principally
I hate and detest that animal called man; although
I heartily love John, Peter, Thomas and so forth.
—JONATHAN SWIFT

ARE YOU an individual, a particular person?

Or are you eager to sink into yourself, which is the
ultimate delusion, or into the group, which is a love of
anonymity? Are you afraid of your difference? If any of
these three questions pertain to you, you are begging for

a great displacement of your most important values by those who benefit from it. For that is the great, glowing goal of the deceivers in our society—to replace your values with theirs so that your life, in the most simple terms, can be manipulated by strings pulled by others.

Only individuality—the expression of your own thoughts into action, pride in your difference and the exercise of that difference—can save you from those who would like to push you into a false, misguided and nonmotivated behavior.

What makes an individualist? The individualist is proud, alert, skeptical, confident, self-aware, definite, objective, subjective, logical, illogical, organic, synthetic, impulsive, meditative, prompt, tardy, practical, impractical, argumentative, docile, direct, roundabout, imaginative, dull, courageous, fearful, sententious, authoritative, lax.

If he seems a bag of paradoxes, he is. If he seems unpredictable, he is. If he offers a problem to pollsters, market researchers and promoters, he is fully capable of giving them king-size headaches. And if he is paradoxical, unpredictable and a headache to the pulse takers and hustlers, he may just be his own man. For if there is one thing that stops a manipulator cold and impels him to test his own reflexes and, incidentally, his own motives and perhaps even his own raison d'être, it is the man or woman who can't be taken for granted because of his or her unpredictability and lack of definable categorization.

Yet even with the clear obstacles that it presents to the value and communications manipulator, individualism is hardly worthy of the stiff backbone that it requires if its pursuit is solely for the sake of confounding the perpetrator. Like the hardy, midwinter swimmer who happily dives into the frigid water, the deliberate individualist must enjoy the inner vigor created by his reactions to the outside world. In that joy, varying on the degree of the individualism, comes self-assurance, happiness, possibly fulfillment and, perhaps an even more important factor, an example to others of a more wavering nature.

Remaining an individual, i.e., being yourself, enjoying the difference but not necessarily viewing the world only from your own boundaries, is simple to describe but difficult to sustain. But it can be sustained by:

*Self-Awareness, or Understanding Yourself and Your Role in Society.* Who are you? What are you in terms of your personal characteristics, educational and professional background and viewpoints, and what are your goals in the world as you see it? How closely, from a realistic standpoint, can you bring them together? Are you being honest in evaluating your progress as both a career seeker and as a human being with obligations to family and community? Have you stopped completing yourself in either of those two roles or is there more that you can achieve in them? Most people find their greatest difficulty is to live fully or to fulfill more than just one of two or three roles—vocation, husband, father, or vocation, wife, mother or whatever the case may be. What's your quota of fulfillment?

*Being Skeptical, Alert and Confident.* "About which the public thinks long it commonly attains to think right," said Samuel Johnson. A healthy skepticism is an obligation you have to yourself. Self-confidence and alertness are obligations you owe everyone, not the least yourself. A fully receptive, dull public, lacking confidence, commitment and viewpoint, is a disaster. Too great a percentage of Americans are drifting in that direction and making it easy and inviting for the deceptions to be committed against them.

In a fictional tour de force published in 1971, *Vandenberg,* written by an anonymous "Oliver Lange," the United States was conquered and occupied by Russia in a surprise attack carefully planned to capitalize on two major traits of Americans. One was their purported blasé and fatheaded acceptance of the ability of the government to withstand invasion and their belief in the cooling of the cold war. The other was their blind acceptance of the country's communications complex. Infiltrators in broadcasting and the press alternately withheld the real news of what was happening and then sent out false versions. A well-conceived, psychological thriller, the novel made a strong impact because of the not-so-hypothetical questions it raised.

*Knowing Your Motivations.* A life style depends considerably on one's economic circumstances but just as much, maybe more, on how one wants to live. Where, how, and when are questions that we all answer many times in our lives on vocation, home and surroundings, and indecisiveness is only a self-delusion. How many people live above their means and how many who can afford to live well choose moderate circumstances instead? Do you want to travel, stay near your hearth or do both? Behavior traits develop a framework for your life style but the character of motivation puts it into motion. So the possibilities are endless for the motivated people

THE WORLD IS FULL OF IT

whose drives and convictions are not easily swayed.

Alfred Adler, often described as the founder of individual psychology, wrote very much to the heart of this matter. "We cannot think, feel or act without the perception of some goal," he observed. "For all the causalities in the world would not suffice to conquer the chaos of the future nor obviate the planlessness to which we would be bound to fall a victim. All activity would persist in the stage of uncontrolled gropings; the economy visible in our psychic life unattained; we should be unintegrated and in every aspect of our physiognomy, in every personal touch, similar to organisms of the rank of the amoeba."

Don't a good many of us lose a grip on our motivations, allow our objectives to grow fuzzy, lose sight of our aims? Whether it pertains to a job, home, or the second car or the sleek boat, or simple self-improvement, or whatever, we find it easy to compromise because no one stands guard on our inner selves. No one but we ourselves and we are easy taskmasters. The biggest gripers I know are those who whiled away their convictions while others exercised theirs.

*Thinking Independently.* Don't let others assume making your decisions for you. This, of course, is the toughest criterion of all. It is all-embracing and determines the rest of them. We tend to accept the judgment of others because we have an inbred fear that we don't know much about anything. Even though proverbially all of us feel we may know a little about a lot and a lot about nothing, deep in each of us we are convinced that it would be possible to be more fully informed on much more if we only had the time and the opportunity. We default on the wish because we fail to make the opportunity and use it as a crutch for the failure.

It's thoroughly possible to be more fully informed. But, in case you expect it, no one can do it for you. It takes effort and some organization. Read more than one newspaper or magazine and don't hesitate to twirl the TV dial. And don't just talk to those people who make you feel comfortable. And always, always, be reasonably skeptical.

Skepticism, of course, can be carried too far. It can become habitual and errant. The individualist is the one who can temper his skepticism with knowledge and information and then make up his opinions by an intelligent reaction. But be wary of an extreme viewpoint, especially your own. You can deceive yourself more easily than anyone can do it for you.

"I recall a professor of philosophy who once consulted me about his cancer phobia," said Carl G. Jung, the highly regarded Swiss psychologist. "He suffered from a compulsive conviction that he had a malignant tumor, although nothing of the kind was ever found in dozens of X-ray pictures. 'Oh, I know there is nothing,' he would say, 'but there *might* be something.' What was it that produced this idea? It obviously came from a fear that was not instilled by conscious deliberation. The morbid thought suddenly overcame him, and it had a power of its own that he could not control.

"It was far more difficult for this educated man to make an admission of this kind than it would have been for a primitive to say that he was plagued by a ghost. The malign influence of evil spirits is at least an admissible hypothesis in a primitive culture, but it is a

© 267

shattering experience for a civilized person to admit that his troubles are nothing more than a foolish prank of the imagination."

The individual who uses reasonable skepticism based on facts, who thinks and acts with independence and follows his own preferences, will not be deceived very often. When it comes to accepting information, it's always wise to keep a corner of your receptiveness open to possible error or falsification. Be a discriminating consumer and you'll eventually have merchants catering to you. Be a discriminating voter and you'll have politicians worrying about what you want. Be a discriminating seeker of culture and entertainment and the quality quotient of television, movies, the theater, literature will eventually benefit.

And so, in the broadest terms, this is what it takes to become an individual and remain one. Can you stand the gaff, name your motivations and stick to your convictions? Will the real *you* please stand up at last?

In outlining some of the criteria for individuality, I reached for the optimum and stated them in imperatives. I do not apologize for it. I can only say that the need for a more aware, more articulate, more discriminating, more militant consumer and citizen is absolutely vital. Without some important measure of individuality and its expression in almost everything we do, we will not only lose our roles as individuals but also lose any claim to our right to be called a society, a term which can be most simply defined as "a voluntary association of individuals for common ends." We will no longer be individuals or have any common ends.

And so—my polemic runs out.

Except for this: If you know the problem despite its complexity, then you've already started solving it and also made it simpler in the process. You are, after all, already in the thick of the battle in a war to be won, a war for the survival of your own identity. And with a prize like that at stake, you can't let *them* continue to deceive you. But they—they who have already been so successful at it—will try, as always.